What does Russia really want from Africa?

Interrogating Russia's re-awakened interest in Africa

Adonis & Abbey Publishers Ltd
Third Floor
207 Regent Street
London W1B 3HH
Website: http://www.adonis-abbey.com
E-mail Address: editor@adonis-abbey.com

Nigeria Office Address:
Unit 1
Vintage Hill Estate
Plot No 1368
Guzape District
Cadastral Zone, A09 FCT.

British Library Cataloguing-in-Publication Data
A catalogue record for this book is available from the British Library

ISBN: 9781913976316

What does Russia really want from Africa?

Interrogating Russia's re-awakened interest in Africa

Jideofor Patrick C. Adibe

ADONIS & ABBEY
PUBLISHERS LTD

Table of Contents

Acknowledgement

This book is a revised version of my Inaugural Lecture presented as the 46th Inaugural Lecture of Nasarawa State University, Keffi, Nigeria on October 30, 2024. I am grateful to the Almighty God for making the Inaugural Lecture possible and successful. I am also grateful to our Vice Chancellor and Chairperson of this occasion, Distinguished Professor Sa'adatu Hassan Liman who was ably represented on the occasion by the Deputy Vice Chancellor (Academic) Professor Abdullahi Sallau Modibbo, who, in 2011 recommended me for employment in the Department when he was the Head of the Department of Political Science. I am equally grateful to the Deputy VC (Administration), Professor Theo Lagi, who, as a former Dean of the Faculty of Social Sciences, was my boss.

I also express my profound gratitude to the following:

- The Registrar of the University, Dr Bala I Ahmed.
- All the Principal Officers of the University—the Provost of the College of Health and Medical Sciences; Dean of the School of Postgraduate School; and other Deans of Faculties, especially the Dean of the Faculty of Social Sciences and former Head of the Department of Political Science, Professor Abdullahi Adadu Yahaya – for his encouragement over the years.
- Professors and other Members of the Senate, especially Eminent Professor S.I. Ibrahim, a former President of the Nigerian Political Science Association, who, as the Dean of the School of Social Sciences in 2011, recommended me for employment in the department.
- Directors of units, institutes, and centres, especially the Director of European Studies, Professor Eugene Aliegba, who was equally a former Head of the Department of Political Science. I thank all heads of departments who graced the occasion, in particular Associate Professor David

Sunday Jacko, the current Head of the Department of Political Science.

I extend my warm greetings to all my colleagues in the department who have been like family to me:

- Professor Shuaibu Ahmed Ibrahim
- Professor Eugene Ternade Aliegba
- Professor Abdullahi Nuhu Liman
- Professor Yahaya Adadu
- Professor George Genyi,
- Professor Abdullahi Yamma
- Professor Modibbo Abdullahi Sallau
- Associate Professor Baban'umma Mohammed Bello
- Associate Professor Canice Esidene Erunke
- Associate Professor Jacho David Sunday
- Associate Professor Ruth Caleb Luka
- Dr Salisu Maikasuwa
- Dr Atsiya Godiya Pius
- Dr Shuaibu Umar Abdul
- Dr AbdullahiMoh'd Abdul
- Dr Solomon Timothy Anjide
- Dr Ugwu Anthony Chinedu
- Dr Philip Ajeh
- Dr Kigbu Dauda Hafsat
- Dr Kana. A.A Ebini
- Dr Aminu Ibrahim
- Dr Yahaya Abubakar Sadiq
- Dr Musa Ibrahim Aliyu
- Dr Usman Gayam Usman
- Dr Onuk Bulus Ojem
- Mr Waibe Ahmadu

I equally thank the department's administrative staff – Hashimu Shuaibu Hashimu, Amina Ismail, Obiajunwa Smart Tochukwu, Happiness Gwangkat, and Abdulmalik Ibrahim.

I also want to thank especially my very beautiful and dedicated wife, Nkem; my children, Adaobi, Udoka, Didi, Zina, and baby Zikora. I thank my mother-in-law as well as my brothers and sisters for their unflinching support.

I am most grateful to Chief Charles Adibe and Ichie Isita Adibe who were my guardians while I was growing up and funded my education from my primary school to the early years of my University education.

I reserve a special place in my heart for eminent Nigerian political scientist Professor J Isawa Elaigwu, my 'oga at the top' who, among other things, facilitated my appointment in the Department of Political Science of the University. I am equally very grateful to former Vice-Chancellor Professor Shamsudeen Amali, who believed in me and offered me a job. Professor Elaigwu also graciously gave a goodwill message at the occasion.

I am equally grateful to those who gave goodwill messages at the occasion – Professor Tunde   former Minister of Education and former Nigeria's Ambassador to the Federal Republic of Germany; Professor Kabiru Isa Dandago, Professor of Accounting at Bayero University Kano and former Commissioner for Finance in the State; Dr Emmanuel Ohakim, Chairman of AMAC MicroFinance Ltd and former Chief of Staff to the Imo State Government; Chief Dennis Anowai, retired Director, Federal Capital Territory Administration's Treasury Department and former President of the Abuja branch of the Ozubulu Development Union (ODU), the umbrella organisation of all indigenes of my town in Abuja, and Dr Ufaruna Sarah Azi, a career Civil Servant and one of the PhD students that I supervised in the Department.

I thank my students; without whom I would not have reached this mileage. I am most grateful to all the ladies and gentlemen who mad out thee the time to grace the occasion – either in person or online.

Preface

How it all began

Inaugural lectures generally are framed to tell the story of one's academic journey embodied in the chosen topic. There are two germane questions here: How did I end up being a Professor of Political Science? And how did I end up doing my inaugural lecture on Russia-Africa relations?

The Young Old Boy Goes to School

I was born in Ibadan Street, Otukpo, on 17 March 1962, to Igbo parents. At the onset of the war, we fled first to Aba, in current Abia State, and then to my home town, Ozubulu, in Ekwusigo Local Government Area of Anambra. I have very little recollection of the early stages of the war, being only about five years old when it began. My earliest recollection of the war was that I was playing with a car tyre when an aeroplane dropped a bomb, and people started running helter-skelter. I had a better recollection of the latter stages of the war when people had to run into one of the numerous bunkers in our village to protect themselves from bombs from fighter planes or when older male relatives had to hide in ceilings or bushes from people forcibly conscripting young men into the Biafran Army.

When the war ended in 1970, it was time for some of us to start school. I started Primary 1 in 1970 as a "young man old boy" of eight years old. In 1972, I moved to Patrick Okolo Memorial Primary School in Onitsha, Anambra State. Thanks to a very creative policy at that time that enabled people from the war-affected East Central State to do two academic years in one calendar year, I was able to conclude my primary education at the right age and got admitted into a secondary school immediately afterwards in 1975/1976. I was within the 13-14 year age band. I was admitted to the University of Nigeria,

Nsukka, in 1980, straight after my secondary school, at the age of 18. I obtained a Master's degree in 1986 at the age of 24 and submitted my PhD thesis in International Development Studies (our equivalent of Political Economy) in 1991 at the age of 29. However, I did not become a full professor until 2017, when I was 55 years old. I think this is an important lesson that the race of life is not necessarily for the swift; when or how we start may not necessarily determine how we finish. Life is a marathon, not a sprint, and we all should be content running in our lane.

How I ended up studying Political Science

My journey to studying political science started at my secondary school, Oraifite Secondary School, Oraifite in Ekwusigo Local Government Area of Anambra State. Political science was not my first option. When we were preparing to sit for our West African School Certificate (WASC) exam in 1980 and the JAMB examination the same year, Political Science was not an option at all, though I was thrilled by the colour and buzz from the campaigns for the 1979 presidential elections in the country, especially by the very bombastic eloquence of people like the late K.O. Mbadiwe (alias Man of Timbre and Calibre), Dr Chuba Okadigbo, Mamman Ali Makele, Uba Ahmed, Ebenezer Babatope, etc.

I believe I was what one could call "a very bright student" in my secondary school days because, as far as I can remember, there were only two occasions from the time I got admitted to the school in 1975/76 as a class one student until I graduated in 1980, that I did not come top of my class. And remember that there were three terms each year in those days, and examinations were held every term. Like many people called 'bright students' in those days, your career path seemed mapped by societal expectations. If you were science-inclined, the societal expectation was that you would become a doctor or an engineer, but if you were inclined to arts subjects, then you were expected to read law. I could easily have taken to the sciences or the arts, as I was pretty good at both. However, medicine, disqualified itself from consideration because I loathed the sight of blood and consequently began gravitating towards the arts. I was active in drama and represented my school severally in school quizzes and debates. This means that as medicine disqualified itself, studying law beckoned. When we got our JAMB forms, I duly chose Law as my first and second choice. I recall that in those days, our English teacher tried to convince me to study English language or English literature at the university. Though I loved both subjects, I secretly wondered how I would tell people that I was studying English at the university, as in those days, it was assumed to be mostly for women or, at best, for average or below-average students, not those you would call "very brilliant students".

Despite knowing I would choose Law as my first and second choice in the JAMB examination, I had an abiding passion for reading novels. A very popular thriller author among my generation of students was James Hadley Chase. It so happened that after I had completed the JAMB form and chosen Law but had not yet submitted the form, I came to read one of Chase's novels I had borrowed from someone from my town. In those days, fans of Hadley Chase novels competed among themselves on the number of his works they had read. His novels had such tantalising titles as *The Way The Cookie Crumbles*, *Have This One on Me*, *Whiff of Money*, etc. We didn't even know that almost all of those novels were published before we were born. There was no Google or social media in those days to help with crosschecking facts. Someone would always tell you of another Chase novel and who had it, and you would search for it in bookshops or from other avid Hadley Chase fans to borrow from them.

13

One of the Hadley Chase novels I borrowed from my townsman was called A *Lotus for Miss Quon*. The main character was Steve Jaffe, an American hustler who discovered two million dollars worth of diamonds hidden in the wall of his villa in Saigon while trying to hang a picture of a Vietnamese dancer on the false wall. His houseboy, Hann, wanted him to return the diamonds to the state, which he promised would reward him with state honours. But Steve Jaffe was not interested in any state honours. He reflected that all his life, he had been dreaming of laying his hands on "big bucks", and then, just when he got the opportunity, his servant was insisting that he should return it for "stupid" state honours. Steve Jaffe tried his best to persuade Hann, even telling him he would sell the gems and give him part of the money to buy a car or get married, but Hann would have none of that. Suddenly, Steve remembered that the man was a supporter of the regime and that for two times a week, he attended courses in political science. Realising that it would be an uphill task to convince Hann, he tried to figure out a way to outwit him and organise an exit visa to leave the country. Suddenly, Hann, not trusting Steve Jaffe, dashed to snatch the bag of gems from his hands and run away. Steve tried to forcefully stop him, but being a much bigger and stronger man, he ended up accidentally strangling him to death.

I was so moved by Mr Hann's patriotism, who, despite being poor, refused to be bribed. I linked his patriotism and incorruptibility to the fact that he was attending courses in political science. From that moment on, my career trajectory changed. I changed my course from law to political science.

I had no difficulty getting admission the same year to the University of Nigeria, Nsukka, to study political science. As an undergraduate student at the UNN, perhaps my biggest passion was to be a published novelist. This was before self-publishing became popular. I wrote so many novels that were unfortunately all rejected by publishers. In about my third year, one of my manuscripts, Fool's Paradise, was published by

Fourth Dimension Publishers, then one of the leading indigenous publishers in the country. I was churning out manuscripts probably at the rate of one every three or four weeks, and they were all constantly rejected by the various publishers I submitted them to.

I graduated in 1984, did my NYSC in 1984/85, and returned to Nsukka for my M.Sc. in 1985/1986, which was completed in 1986, just one year after I registered for the programme - a record in those days. I registered for a PhD at the same university in 1987 but left the country for Denmark in 1988. I submitted my PhD thesis in 1991 to Roskilde University (which was regarded as the most radical university in Denmark in those days), but did my viva several months later, in 1992. Essentially, from the time I started primary school in 1970 at the grand 'young-old age' of 8 years (because of the disruptions of the Civil War) to the time I submitted my PhD thesis in 1991, I had spent about 21 uninterrupted years in school.

While studying in Denmark, I was lucky to work as a full-time Guest Research Fellow at the Centre for Development Research, Copenhagen, Denmark. Structural adjustment was a popular topic then because almost all sub-Saharan African countries were implementing one form of IMF/World Bank-supported structural adjustment programme or the other. At that time, terminologies like "conditionalities" and "cross-conditionalities" were common because implementing an IMF/World Bank-supported Structural Adjustment Programme was a condition for many countries to reschedule their debts or obtain new letters of credit. At the CDR, I was part of the team that examined the impact of the IMF/World Bank-supported structural adjustment programmes on agriculture in Africa. My PhD thesis was on 'State and the Peasantry: Farmers' Responses to the Structural Adjustment Programme in Nigeria'.

Academic Identity Crisis

In November 1994, I went for a post-doctoral programme at the Centre for Developing Area Studies, McGill University, Montreal, Canada. This was the time when the Internet was emerging. While there, I met many young professionals from the USA who had nice-looking complimentary cards that read 'Internet Consultant'. Being an 'Internet Consultant' in those days was mostly about teaching people how to surf the Internet using the then-popular browser, Internet Explorer, or the new graphics-based Microsoft programmes, such as Word, Excel, PowerPoints, and Visual Basics. The new graphics-based office packages were just replacing the DOS-based versions and electric typewriters. Using such Microsoft programmes meant you were on the top curve of the IT revolution. It was while I was a Guest Research Fellow at the Centre for Development Research (CDR) in Copenhagen, Denmark, that I had my first Computer— a Commodores. In those days, you don't just turn on your computer and start using it. First, you needed to upload the operating system using up to ten diskettes (depending on whether you were using 51/4" or the 3 1/2" types). I recall that when one researcher from the UK visited the CDR as a Guest Research Fellow, he came with a computer (I think it was an Amstrad), which had a hard disc of 20 megabytes. That meant he did not need to load the operating system with multiple diskettes before using his computer. We saw him like a guy from the Silicon Valley.

Given that I had spent about 21 unbroken years as a student between 1970 (when I was enrolled as a Primary 1 student and 1991 (when I first submitted my PhD thesis) and that I was dealing with virtually the same concepts as a Guest Research fellow at both the CDR, the NORDISKA, and as a post-doctoral fellow at the Centre for Developing Areas Studies (CDAS), McGill, I began to develop an academic identity crisis bordering on whether I was right to study political science in the first place, and whether I was right in putting myself on the path to an academic career.

When I returned from Canada to Denmark in 1995, I sought and obtained admission at the University of Kent in Canterbury, United Kingdom, to study for an M.Sc. (conversion) programme in Computer Science. Unfortunately, it did not go well because I could not figure out Pascal programming.

Later, I took a CATS Points accredited short course on the New Economic Powers (Brazil, Russia, India, and China) from the Department of Continuing Education, Oxford University, United Kingdom, from September 2007 to December 2007. At that time, South Africa had not become bracketed into the group (it only became a group member in 2010). It should be recalled that BRIC, as an acronym, was coined in 2001 by the then Goldman Sachs' chief economist, Jim O'Neill, in a research paper that underlined the growth potential of the four countries. There was a big buzz around the grouping then following those forecasts. However, it was only in 2009 that the grouping began to evolve as an informal club, mostly as an initiative of Russia.

Between September 2007 and October 2009, I did an LLM programme in Media Law at the City University, London. My dissertation, which was on 'Free Speech v. Reputation: Public Interest Defence in American and English Law of Defamation', was scored an 'A'.

Setting up Adonis & Abbey Publishers—the road to a teaching job at Nasarawa State University

I relocated from Denmark to the United Kingdom in 1998. While living and working there, I felt I was done with academics. I worked mostly for a media monitoring company—Prominent Pages (later taken over by a bigger monitoring company called Durrants). I was a regular contributor to a popular monthly magazine known as *NewAfrican*. I also resurrected my ambition of being a novelist. From an insider at Heinemann's African Writers' Series, where I submitted the manuscript of a novel I called *Broken Dream*, I was informed that it received good reviews and had good prospects of being published. It seemed it was just a matter of time before I would receive an acceptance letter. However, when I eventually got a letter from Heinemann, it was to tell me that the manuscript had been rejected. To say I was devastated would be, to put it mildly.

Dejected and deflated, I decided to visit Baffour Ankomah, the Ghanaian editor of the *New African* in his office in Central London. During our conversation, I mentioned in passing that I was planning to set up a book publishing company. The following month, the magazine published a story on its inside back page cover with the caption, "New Hope for African Writers." Baffour Ankomah had more confidence in me than I had in myself. On March 18, 2003, a new publishing company, Adonis & Abbey Publishers, was born, and the original aim was to publish works of fiction.

After the first novel, *Broken Dreams,* which was the one I thought Heinemann's AWS was to publish, destiny took its turn. Baffour Ankoma introduced me to another regular contributor to the *NewAfrican*, an Ethiopian scholar and Africanist called Mammo Muchie, whom I often called 'The Lion of Judah' because of the regal manner he carried himself. This was during the period of intense Afro-pessimism in Europe, and one particular newspaper in the UK had caricatured the idea of the 'African renaissance' that was being promoted by Thabo Mbeki in South Africa by mockingly asking when Africa ever had its 'renaissance'. In our contributions to the *New African* magazine, we sought, in various ways, to challenge notions and innuendos that ruled out both development and democratic possibilities for Africa. Remarkably, the second book published by Adonis & Abbey

Publishers was an edited book by Mammo Muchie, which was defiantly entitled *The Making of the Africa-Nation: Pan Africanism and the African Renaissance*. In 2004, we set up a journal called African *Renaissance*, which was semi-academic and published every other month. Part of the avowed mission of the journal was "to let African scholars set their own agenda for research rather than constantly anticipating the needs of the funding agencies that usually fund these journals". We got several Africanists—Kwesi Prah in South Africa, Jamal Nkrumah (Kwame Nkrumah's son) from Egypt, Helmi Sharawy, Marcel Kitissou, Chinweizu (Nigeria), etc.—to contribute regularly. We did a special issue on Zimbabwe and interviewed people from its High Commission in London to hear its own side of the story because at that time the country was a pariah in the United Kingdom. In fact, a prominent cabinet minister under Tony Blair's government nearly lost his job for shaking the hands of the Zimbabwean President at that time, Robert Mugabe. His saving grace was that he claimed that the place was dark, and he did not know it was Mugabe who stretched out his hand for a handshake.

Meeting Ali Mazrui, being introduced to Professor Elaigwu, and securing a teaching appointment at NSUK

Professor Ali Mazrui, the late Kenyan-American political scientist, was one of the most important persons Mammo Muchie introduced to me. Mammo Muchie gave me Professor Mazrui's number and suggested that he might be interested in the sort of intellectual engagements we were pursuing at the time.

There was an incident the first day I called Professor Ali Mazrui. He was a very well-known scholar—at least among African political scientists. A documentary history he wrote and narrated in the early 1980s, jointly produced by the BBC and the Public Broadcasting Service (WETA, Washington) in association with the Nigerian Television Authority, further made him a household name. A book by the same title was co-published by BBC Publications and Little, Brown and Company. The film series premiered in 1986 on BBC and local PBS stations throughout the United States. To put it mildly, Professor Mazrui's reputation was huge.

Given his global stature, I was not exactly full of confidence that an obscure public intellectual like me, who had set up a nondescript publishing company and was publishing an unknown journal, would get much of his attention. Surprisingly, when I called the number, expecting that if he picked up at all, he would be so busy that he wouldn't give me more than a few seconds, he was quite generous with his time.

I told him about his books. I had read and proudly recited some of the quotations I memorised from those books. However, rather irreverently, I told him I didn't like his allegorical work, *The Trial of Christopher Okigbo* (1972). I told him that I threw away the book in disgust after reading it. Christopher Okigbo was a well-respected Igbo poet who, at the beginning of the Nigerian Civil War, opted to fight on the side of Biafra. In a fictional Hereafter, Ali Mazrui tried and convicted him for subordinating his art to his community.

Mazrui was silent for a while and then asked if I thought I was old enough to understand the book's message since I said I read it in my early years as an undergraduate when I was still a teenager. I argued that it was wrong for Okigbo to be found guilty in the Hereafter because a writer's community preceded his art and that a writer who subordinates his art to his community is only indulging in "arts for arts' sake". There was a long silence through which my pounding heart told me I had blown the opportunity. When Mazrui finally spoke, it was to give me his home telephone number and asked me to call at my convenience. This was quintessential Mazrui—humble and tolerant of criticisms in a way his critics never were. In 2009, Professor Mazrui wrote the 'Preface' to a book I edited and also contributed two chapters to the book. The book, titled, *Who is an African? Identity, Citizenship, and the Making of the Africa-Nation* was very well received.

Mazrui later became the editorial adviser to the *African Renaissance*. Adonis & Abbey Publishers, our publishing company, also became his preferred European publisher. Additionally, Mazrui introduced me to his former student, eminent Nigerian political scientist Professor J. Isawa Elaigwu, and we became quite close. When I finally relocated to Nigeria, it was Professor Elaigwu who insisted that I needed an "academic address" and in 2011 facilitated my employment as a lecturer in the Department of Political Science of this great university. I was employed as a senior lecturer on September 1, 2011. I became an Associate Professor in 2014 and a full Professor in 2017.

After Professor Mazrui passed away on 12 October 2014, I was appointed a co-editor of a book of worldwide tribute in his honour. The book, entitled, *A Giant Tree Has Fallen: Tributes to Ali Al'Amin Mazrui* was published in 2016 by African Perspectives in South Africa. A year after his death, Twaweza Communications of Kenya and the Binghamton University of New York (where Professor Mazrui taught) organised a symposium entitled 'Critical Perspectives on Culture and Globalisation: The Intellectual Legacy of Ali A Mazrui.' The symposium, held in Nairobi, Kenya, from July 14-17, 2015, attracted nearly 100 Africanists from all over the world. I was among the three Nigerian Africanists invited to the symposium. The other two were eminent Nigerian political scientist J. Isawa Elaigwu, who chaired a session and also gave the concluding remarks at the symposium; Prof. Adekeye Adebajo, who presented a paper on 'Who Killed Pax Africana?' and my humble self, who presented a paper on 'Who is an African? Reflections on Mazrui's notion of the African. '.My presentation also appeared as a chapter in a book with the same title as the symposium's theme, published in 2017 by Twaweza Communications of Kenya.

Why I Chose to Give my Inaugural Lecture on Russo-Africa Relations

In 2013, I was part of a four-man team commissioned by the Africa Growth Initiative at the Brookings Institution to study the impact of conflicts on agriculture in Nigeria and Mali. Of these four, two were from Nigeria (Abigail Jirgi, an agricultural scientist, and my humble self, a political scientist). The other two were from Mali—one political scientist and an agricultural scientist. Between April 14 and 15, 2014, we presented our findings at Brookings' headquarters in Washington, DC. I think my presentation found favour with some of the members of the Africa Growth Initiative because I was asked to write for the 2015 edition of *Foresight Africa*, the highly regarded annual flagship report on Africa by the Brookings Institution.

When the article entitled 'The 2015 Presidential Elections in Nigeria: The Issues and Challenges' was published (just months before the 2015 presidential elections), it caused a big stir in the country. Many newspapers supporting the PDP and President Goodluck Jonathan had it on the front page under headlines such as "Brookings Tips Jonathan to Win". The then-opposition APC went after the Brookings Institution and me. Some tried to minimise the supposed impact of that article (which, by the way, never really claimed that President Jonathan would win but merely emphasised the difficulty of defeating an incumbent African President) by emphasising that the article was not actually from Brookings but by a scholar "from obscure Nasarawa State University". For several months, the article held the record of being the most read on the Brookings website. Consequently, I became one of the few privileged scholars to have a dedicated blog on the Brookings website because the think-tank encouraged me to write for them on several other issues.

One of the issues I wrote for them was on the First Russia-Africa Summit, held on 23–24 October 2019 in Sochi, Russia, which was co-hosted by Russian President Vladimir Putin and Egyptian President Abdel Fattah el-Sisi. As many as 43 heads of state or government attended the summit. I entitled my piece, 'What Does Russia Really Want from Africa?" and it was published on November 14, 2019, on the Brookings website—after the usual robust reviews. Largely because the Brookings Institution is one of the most respected think-tanks in the world, and given the rigour that goes into the review of any piece they publish, whatever they publish is usually guaranteed a global audience. Therefore, it was not surprising that the article attracted much interest, including interviews from many international media houses.

In 2021, I was invited by Chatham House, another well-respected think-tank, to present at a Zoom Workshop it organised on July 15 of that year on Russia-Sub-Saharan Africa's Relations. I titled my presentation, 'What is Driving Russia's Renewed Interest in Africa?' In 2022, I was again invited by the Bristol-based E-International Relations (www.https://www.e-ir.info), generally regarded as the leading international relations platform in the world, to write on the impact of the Russo-Ukraine war on Africa and to project on the likely configuration of the world after the war and Africa's location in it. I entitled my piece 'The Russo-Ukrainian War's Impact: Africa and a 'Neo-Cold War', published as an open-access article on December 20, 2022.

Given that I am a Professor of International Relations, the topic also offers an opportunity to illustrate and synthesise my thoughts on various aspects of International Relations, International Economic Relations, and Foreign Policy Analysis. For instance, discussing the economic impact of the Russo-Ukraine war on Africa is also an excursion into International Economic Relations, big power politics (and their use of proxies in their struggles for hegemony and spheres of influence) as well as understanding the consequences of the globalization of markets on Africa. In fact, my initial title for the inaugural lecture was "Africa in the Clutches of Big Power Politics: A Case Study of Russo-Africa Relations". I later abandoned this for the current title, which I feel is shorter, more contemporaneous, and likely to attract more attention. However, the goal remains the same: to use it as a subtext to tell the story of my academic journey, especially as a Professor of International Relations.

Methodology and theoretical framework

I relied mostly on secondary sources of information to gather my materials—books, journals, internet blogs, and newspaper articles. For analysis of the materials, I relied on content analysis of the gathered materials and using both inductive and deductive reasoning to arrive at conclusions.

The narration uses a historical approach and draws from such theoretical frames as the Truman Doctrine, which was enunciated by President Harry Truman in 1947 and which made it obligatory for the US to contain Soviet expansionism anywhere. For the section on what Russia really wants from Africa and the impact of the Russo-Ukraine war on Africa, I drew inspiration from Robert Keohane and Joseph Nye's complex interdependence theory of the 1970s, where, in their neoliberal critique of the realist view of the world, they argued that international politics is transformed by interdependence and that the fortunes and even misfortunes of both state and non-state actors are often inextricably tied together.

My Academic Profile

I began my academic journey at the Wesley College of Education, Ibadan, where I did my NYSC in 1984/1985. I was a guest research fellow at the Centre for Development in

Copenhagen, Denmark, for about four years (while doing my PhD and about another year after). I was a guest research fellow at the Nordic Institute for African Affairs (Nordiska) in Uppsala, Sweden. I did my post-doctoral studies at the Centre for Developing Area Studies, McGill University, Montreal, Canada. I started full-time teaching at the Department of Political Science at Nasarawa State University, Keffi, on September 1, 2011.

1. *Number of post-graduate students graduated*: about 15 PhDs and at least 25 M.Sc.

2. Scholarly influence

- H-Index as of 28/09/24 was 16: (ranked No. 3 in the university by the AD Scientific Index)
- i10 Index: 23 as of 28/09/24: (Ranked No.3 in the University according to AD Scientific Index).
- Total Google Scholar citations: 778 as of September 28, 2024, with over 99% being single-authored works. The AD Scientific Index ranked me as the most cited scholar in the Department of Political Science and the Faculty of the Social Sciences and among the top ten most cited scholars in the university.

3. In the past 12 years, more than 70% of my invitations to seminars, workshops, or symposia had been as the lead speaker or as the lead discussant.
4. I have published over 80 academic articles and 10 books either as a sole author, editor, or co-editor.

5. *Editor-in-Chief* of two high-impact academic journals:

(a) *Journal of African Union Studies*. The journal, a triennial high-impact academic journal, was founded in 2012 and focuses on the study of the African Union as an institution, its 8 Regional Economic Communities, and other multilateral or bi-national commissions in the continent that promote the goal of the AU. It is indexed in most of the world's leading global databases, including SCOPUS, IBSS, JSTOR, ERIH Plus, ProQuest, EBSCO, and SABINET. It is accredited by DHET (the regulator of higher education in South Africa) and UGC CARE (the regulator of higher education in India).

(b) African Journal of Terrorism and Insurgency Research: The journal, a bi-annual, high-impact academic journal, was founded in 2020 and is indexed in several of the world's leading databases, including ProQuest, EBSCO, and SABINET. It is listed in the Norwegian List (also known as The Register for Scientific Journals, Series, and Publishers), an official Norwegian list consisting of publication channels considered scientific. The list is operated jointly by the National Board of Scholarly Publishing (NPU) and the Norwegian Directorate for Higher Education and Skills on behalf of the Norwegian Ministry of Education and Research.

6. *Extraordinary Professor*, School of Government Studies of the North-West University, Mahikeng Campus, South Africa, since October 2022.

7. Guest Lecturer, National Defence College, Abuja, since February 2023.

8. External examiner, University of Kwazulu, Natal,

9. Community service

- Consultant to the National Peace Committee during the 2015 presidential election.
- Vice Chairman, National Peace and Harmony Council, a think-tank (since early 2024)
- Was a back-page columnist for the Daily Trust newspaper for ten years (2010-2020) every Thursday. I am also a syndicated columnist for Premium Times, The Vanguard, and The News Chronicle every Tuesday.

- Except CNN, I have been interviewed by most of the world's leading media houses: BBC, Pravda (Russia), AFP (Agence France-Presse), Reuters, Danmark Radio (Denmark), CBC, Radio Free Europe, etc. I am a fairly regular face on such Nigerian news channels as Arise, Channels, and AIT.
- I founded Adonis & Abbey Publishers in the UK in 2003. In addition to publishing nearly 200 books, it also publishes 27 high-impact academic journals, 7 of which are indexed by SCOPUS and ranked by SCImago Journal Ranking. It is a publishing partner with Web of Science for its Book Citation Index (BKCI). Two of the company's journals are ranked Q2 by SCImago, while two of its books are indexed by Web of Science in its Book Citation Index (BKCI).

Below are two quotes about Adonis & Abbey Publishers by scholarly studies on what is now called 'bibliometric economy' or 'bibliometric coloniality'.

By having a London base, by publishing work by academics based in Nigeria and across the Nigerian diaspora, and by ensuring global distribution and indexing, Adonis and Abbey has managed to bridge the local–global gap. It is a gap that other Nigerian journals and presses struggle to cross.
By David Mills and Abigail Branford (2022), in "Getting By in a Bibliometric Economy: Scholarly Publishing and Academic Credibility in the Nigerian Academy", published in the journal, Africa (Cambridge University Press), p. 853

But our book shows how African researchers, editors and publishers are finding creative ways of not only 'getting by' but also developing a global scholarly reputation. Examples include Adonis & Abbey publishers, based in Nigeria and the UK, publishing journals that are indexed in a range of global databases, the Council for the Development of Social Science Research in Africa based in Senegal (CODESRIA) with a pan-African reputation for its social science journals, and Hindawi, started by two Egyptian researchers in Cairo in 1997, and which became a global 'top-10' journal publisher before being acquired by Wiley in January 2021 for US$300 million.

Cited in the review of the book: Who Counts? Ghanaian academic publishing and global science, published by African Minds in 2023 and reviewed by Wagdy Sawahel under the title "Escaping 'bibliometric coloniality', 'epistemic inequality'", in World University News (African edition), on 15 February, 2023.

https://www.universityworldnews.com/post.php?story=20 230213021356132

Chapter One: Introduction

The Evolution of Russo-Africa Relations

Early contacts between Russia and African countries can be traced to the late 18th century when the Russian Empire sought support from the rulers of Morocco, Egypt, and Tunisia in its confrontation with the Ottoman Empire. Following this, diplomatic relations were established with Tunisia as early as 1869, followed by Morocco in 1897, Ethiopia in 1898, and later with the Boer Republic of Transvaal (Tass, 2023).

Russia-Africa relations became low-keyed after the October Revolution of 1917 in Russia, even though the socialist revolution in the country appeared to have inspired some socialist groups in Africa. For instance, in the 1930s, we had the Algerian Communist Party, which was an important faction of the Algerian nationalist movement, though it curiously supported France in the growing unrest of the time and was forced to dissolve in 1956. Activists in the party later joined the militant National Liberation Front and actively participated in the ferocious Algerian War of Independence of the 1950s. During that war of independence, Moscow provided military, technical, and material assistance to the FLN and trained hundreds of its military leaders in the USSR. The Soviet Union also became the first country in the world to recognise the Provisional Government of the Algerian Republic in 1962 by establishing diplomatic relations a few months before the official proclamation of its independence (Ruedy, 1992). Similarly, the Communist International (Comintern, also known as the Third International), an international organisation founded in 1919 that advocated world communism and which was led and controlled by the Communist Party of the Soviet Union, included the declaration of solidarity for the "colonial slaves of Africa and Asia". In fact, Vladimir Lenin, the founder of Soviet communism, argued in his book, *Imperialism: The Highest Stage of Capitalism* (1917), that imperialism is driven by the quest for capital accumulation. By doing so, he could establish a theoretical link between the anti-colonial struggles in the colonies and the struggles against capitalism in the Soviet Union.

Egypt was the first African country with which the USSR signed a trade treaty (1955), followed by Tunisia (1957), Morocco (1958), Ghana, Ethiopia, and Guinea (all in 1959). In 1960, Moscow established the Patrice Lumumba Peoples' Friendship University to provide higher education to students from developing countries. The university was named after Patrice Émery Lumumba (born Isaïe Tasumbu Tawosa), the first prime minister of the Democratic Republic of the Congo (then known as the Republic of the Congo) from June until September 1960. Lumumba, who was the leader of the Congolese National Movement (MNC) from 1958 until his execution in January 1961, is generally regarded as a martyr for the Pan-African movement. Critics have, however, argued that Patrice Lumumba University became an integral part of the Soviet cultural offensive in Africa (Rubinstein, 1971, cited in Wikipedia).

Egypt

Egypt under Gamal Abdel Nasser in the 1950s was known for its anti-imperialist and socialist inclinations. Under Nasser, many young Egyptians studied in Soviet universities and military schools, including Hosni Mubarak, who was to later become the country's president. Mubarak trained in a military pilot school at Kant Air Base, Kyrgyzstan. After the death of Nasser, Anwar Sadat, who succeeded him, began reorienting the country towards the West. In fact, in September 1981, Saddat accused the Soviet Union of trying to undermine his government because of the Egypt-Israeli Peace Treaty, which was signed on 26 March 1979, following the 1978 Camp David

Accords. Relations between the two countries deteriorated sharply but were re-established under Hosni Mubarak in 1984.

Ethiopia

In Ethiopia, a 1974 military coup led by General Mengistu Haile Mariam installed the Derg, a Communist-leaning junta that became a close ally of the Soviet Union. Moscow probably wanted to use that alliance to prove that a society as backwards as Ethiopia could become revolutionary by embracing its Communist ideology. Soviet support of the Mengistu government, however, infuriated the government of Siad Barre in Somalia, which was also pro-communist and which had earlier rejected a proposal by Moscow for a four-nation Marxist-Leninist confederation in the Horn of Africa. During the Ogaden War (also known as the Ethio-Somali War), Soviet support for Ethiopia played a crucial role in turning the tide of the war against Somalia, which was on the verge of victory before Mengistu requested Soviet assistance. The then USSR sent munitions such as fighter bombers, tanks, and artillery (Oberdorfer, 1978). Somalia was so infuriated by the Soviet support for Ethiopia that it annulled its treaty with the country and expelled all the Soviet advisers.

South Africa

In 1896, the Transvaal Republic established diplomatic relations with Russia, whose media had extensively covered the Boer War, with many Russians wishing that the Boers would defeat the arrogant British. It was said that popular support for the Boers was so great that many inns, restaurants, and cafés were given Afrikaans names (Willers, 2023). After South Africa became a republic in 1961, relations between the two countries were largely cold. South Africa had an unfavourable view of the Soviet Union because it believed the country provided both financial and military support to many anti-government and Communist groups in the country. In fact, South Africa severed ties with Moscow in 1956 because of its alleged support for the South African Communist Party. In the same vein, South Africa accused the Soviet Union of training combat units from Namibia (SWAPO members) and Angola (MPLA) at the military training camp of the African National Congress in Tanzania during the long-drawn South African Border War between 1966 and 1990. The Soviet Union also openly supported the ANC during the Apartheid days in the country, even though it was at the same time also surreptitiously involved in trade with the Apartheid government, mostly in arms and mineral resources (Plaut, 2018). For instance, between 1960 and 1964, the South African mining giant De Beers contracted to market Russia's diamond from Siberia. However, in May 1964, the South African diamond cartel stopped selling Soviet diamonds on world markets because Moscow supported a lot of trade with South Africa (New York Times, 1964). These sanctions were, however, being busted variously. For instance, in the 1980s, the South African military group Armscor had a team of experts working in Leningrad who were involved in jet engine development (Van Vurren, 2018; Plaut, 2018). Diplomatic relations between Russia and South Africa were re-established in February 1992, after the Soviet Union was dissolved.

Nigeria

Nigeria and the then Soviet Union established diplomatic relations on November 2, 1960, barely a month after the country gained independence in 1960. Despite this, Nigeria's Prime Minister Tafawa Balewa had a decidedly pro-Western inclination and was said to have assured the British government that "we shall use every means in our power to prevent the infiltration of communism and communist ideas into Nigeria" (cited in Husain, 2024). Segun Odunuga, said to be the first Professor of Russian Studies in Africa, and one of the early beneficiaries of Russian scholarship to African students was quoted as saying: "The Nigerian government didn't want people to go to Russia at the time. Russia was not the place to go then. In fact, it was after I got to Moscow that I wrote to my father to inform him that I was in Moscow. Incidentally, just before the postman came to deliver my parcel, a CID man (Criminal Investigative Department) was there interrogating my father on my whereabouts" (cited in Adetokunbo, 2017).

During the country's Civil War (1967-1970), Soviet military assistance to the country at a time when its traditional allies like Britain were hesitant to supply it with weapons marked a watershed in the relations between the two countries. This led to a deepening of the relations between the two countries, with several Russian products being imported into the country and several lucrative contracts in diverse areas such as metallurgy and petroleum industries, geological prospecting, public health services, and personnel training awarded to the country. More than 15 joint agreements were signed during this period, including the agreement on air communication in 1967, the agreement on economic, scientific, and technical cooperation in 1968, an agreement on cultural cooperation in 1970 and a trade agreement in 1987, an agreement on cooperation against narcotics in 1990, and Russia's technical assistance in the geological prospecting works on metallurgical raw materials: iron ore, coal, and non-metallic raw materials (Adetokunbo, 2017, 481-482).

One of the mega contracts Russia secured was the Ajaokuta Steel Company, which was dubbed the "bedrock of Nigeria's industrialisation". It stood as the symbol of Nigeria's dream of greatness, modernity, and prosperity. The project spans 24,000 hectares (59,305 acres), almost the size of the

Maldives islands in the Indian Ocean, and includes the 800-hectare plant. The Russian contractor Tyajz Prom Export (TPE) started construction in 1979. At that time, it was estimated to cost between $6 billion and $10 billion. Former Nigerian President Olusegun Obasanjo rationalised the choice of Russia for the contract thus:

> In my first presidency, there was the general belief that steelmaking was at the heart of industrialisation. India had built the first steel plant with Russian help, and they built their second almost without help. We thought we needed to achieve that, but we did not have enough money to do it alone. So, we went to the Soviet Union, and there we obtained the best deal on offer: we got a free loan from the Russian government, and we commissioned an experienced Soviet contractor, TPE, to design and build the plant (cited in Yemi, 2023).

TPE was originally expected to complete the project by 1983. The company was said to have a track record of on-schedule, on-cost delivery of steel projects, including in Brazil, South Korea, and China.

While the Soviets focused on the steel mill, Western contractors had to be found for the civil works. However, disputes arose, with the Soviets withholding personnel because their accommodation had not been built. There was also tension between Russian and Nigerian workers because the Russians were perceived to be receiving unfairly astronomical salaries and other benefits to their detriment. Largely because of these issues, delays and overruns accumulated. By the time Shehu Shagari, who began the project, was removed in a military coup in 1983, the project was 84% completed, and despite other challenges, the steel mill was said to have reached 98% completion in 1994, with 40 of the 43 plants at the facility having been built (Oluyole, 2017).

When Olusegun Obasanjo returned to power as a civilian president in 1999, he wanted to revive the Ajaokuta Steel

Company, but the Soviet Union, the previous partner to the project, was no longer in existence, having been dissolved after the collapse of the Soviet Union in 1991. In 2002, the Obasanjo government concessioned the project to Japanese Kobe Steel, but it did not quite work out. In 2004, the project was to Ispat Industries in a deal financed by Global Infrastructure Holdings Limited (GIHL) (now Global Steel Holdings Limited, GSHL), which is chaired by Indian steel magnate Pramod Mittal. The Yar'Adua government, which succeeded Obasanjo, ended the concession in 2008 after accusing GIHL of asset stripping. The company sued Nigeria at the International Chamber of Commerce. The dispute was initially resolved in 2016, with Nigeria regaining control of the Ajaokuta Steel Mill in exchange for GIHL retaining the Nigerian Iron Ore Mining Company (NIOMCO) operating at Itakpe. However, in 2022, the Nigerian government paid $496 million to GSHL to settle the claims (Izuaka, 2022).

In October 2019, President Buhari and Russian President Vladimir Putin met at the Russia-Africa Summit in Sochi and agreed to revive the steel mill. In August 2024, it was reported that a team of 23 Russian engineers had arrived at Ajaokuta Steel Company to commence an extensive assessment of the company after years of neglect as part of the efforts to revive the moribund industrial hub (Natsa, 2024).

Chapter Two: Russia-Africa Summits

The First Russia-Africa Summit

The first Russo-Africa summit was held in Sochi, Russia, from October 23–25, 2019. During the summit, Russia welcomed 43 African heads of state or government, along with dozens of business and community leaders. The Summit ended with the usual optics: it spawned $12.5 billion in business deals, largely in arms and grains. The Kremlin also unveiled plans to double trade with African countries to $40 billion per annum (Paquette, 2019). African leaders also had loads of photo-ops with Russian President Vladimir Putin, and as part of the razzmatazz, there were reminders in some media that Russia never colonised any part of Africa and that it was the Soviet leader Khrushchev, who, at the XV General Assembly of the United Nations, moved a motion for African countries under colonialism to be granted independence by 1960 (Adibe, 2019).

Another reportage that fitted the mood of the moment during the summit was the highlighting of the narrative that Russia emphasises collaboration over aid in its relations with Africa and, by implication, respects Africans more than the continent's traditional allies, who are often criticised for being patronising or condescending towards the continent. For instance, in his book, *Manufacturing Hate: How Africa Was Demonised in Western Media* (2021), Milton Allimadi traces the history of the demonisation of Africa and, by extension descendants of Africa in Western media—books, newspapers, and magazines—from the 17th century to our contemporary era. There are several books on how Africans feel they are disrespected or exploited by their traditional allies, essentially the West. The compelling reads in this genre include Walter Rodney's *How Europe Underdeveloped Africa* (1972), Chinweizu's The West and the Rest of Us: White Predators, Black Slavers, and the African Elite (1975), and Joseph R. Gibson's *How Europe and America Are Still Under-developing Africa: Neocolonialism and the Scramble for Strategic Resources in 21st Century Africa* (2021). Beyond the splashy show of unity and camaraderie of newly-found love at Sochi, the first Russo-Africa summit also raised several speculations and very interesting questions: One fundamental issue raised by the Russia-Africa Summit was how Africa's traditional allies, especially the United States, would respond to Russia's 'newfound' love for the continent. The concern of some Africanists at that time was whether Russia's newfound love for Africa would lead to a revival of the 'Truman Doctrine' (Kaine, 2017). This was a pronouncement by President Harry S. Truman on March 12, 1947, offering immediate economic and military aid to the governments of Greece (which was threatened by communist insurrection) and Turkey (which was under pressure from Soviet expansion in the Mediterranean area). This speech, often used by historians to date the beginning of the Cold War, essentially meant that whenever Russia moved in, America's interest was automatically awakened to contain it. The big question, therefore, was whether, with the media glare of the Russia-Africa Summit, America would, in a knee-jerk manner, activate the Truman doctrine.

Though the Cold War is all over now, however, with Russia beginning to re-assert itself globally since Putin's presidency (and even being a big issue in the 2019 presidential election in the USA), there were fears that America might be forced to take more than a passing notice of Russia's seemingly new love overtures to the continent. Some feared that following the Truman Doctrine, America and its allies might try to surreptitiously undermine any Russia-Africa initiative they perceived as a threat. However, the First Russo-Africa Summit and Russia's projection of power on the global stage at that time also presented Nigeria and other African countries with the opportunity to play the two powers against each other for their own benefit, as they did during the Cold War. For instance, when America was dilly-dallying about selling arms to the country to fight Boko Haram, the country turned to a willing Russia and was able to place an order for 12 Mi-35 attack helicopters (Reuters, 2019).

What was specifically at the Russia-Africa summit for Nigeria? Garba Shehu, President Buhari's Senior Special Assistant on Media at the time, gave a long list of takeaways from Buhari's attendance at the summit. These include (Shehu, 2019):

(a) The Russians agreed to a government-to-government understanding that would see them return to complete the Ajaokuta Steel Rolling Mill, (which was abandoned after it had gulped over USD 5 billion without it coming to fruition);

(b) The Russian railway giant, MEDPROM, indicated interest in undertaking the 1,400-kilometre Lagos-Calabar rail track that will pass through all the states in the South-South sub-region.

(c) An MOU was signed between the NNPC and Russia's oil giant Lukoil to upgrade their commercial relationship to a government-to-government-backed partnership to enable them to work together in upstream operations and in revamping Nigeria's ill-functioning refineries.

(d) Buhari assured Putin that the protracted issue of the Aluminium Smelter Company of Nigeria, ALSCON, at Ikot-Abasi, Akwa-Ibom State (which is owned by the Russian company AC RUSA but dogged by many problems, including protracted legal challenges), would be resolved.

Reading the press on Buhari's 'mission accomplished' visit to Sochi, one would get the wrong impression that Buhari returned with a bagful of investments. The truth is that an MOU does not guarantee that an investment will happen. In fact, most of the promises in the various Africa Summits (including the one organised by President Obama in the USA in 2014) hardly deliver on their promises and appear to be geared more towards optics than anything else. Let us not forget that in 2009, the Russian President at the time, Dmitri Medvedev, visited Nigeria as part of a four-nation Africa tour that included Egypt, Angola, and Namibia. During the visit, Medvedev was reportedly accompanied by a business delegation numbering 400, including the heads of major Russian companies, such as Gazprom and Alrosa. An agreement was reportedly signed between the Nigerian National Petroleum Company and Gazprom to develop two gas fields and work on the feasibility of the trans-Sahara pipeline. It was believed that Russia's involvement in its construction and operation would give the country yet another lever to achieve its objective of controlling access to gas used in central and western Europe (Wheeler, 2009). It may be tempting to question what really became of that accord. In fact, some years after the Sochi meeting, it is easy to look at the deals, the MOUs signed, and the promises made and be able to interrogate how many of such were ever realised.

The Second Russia-Africa Summit

The Second Russo-Africa Summit, which was originally scheduled to be held at the African Union headquarters in Addis Ababa, Ethiopia, on October 20, 2022, was eventually held at the Expo Forum in St. Petersburg, Russia's second-largest city after Moscow, on July 27 and 28, 2023. The original idea of holding it in Addis Ababa was partly in response to criticisms of African leaders being herded into one European or American capital in the name of the Africa Summit–like small boys. The venue was shifted to Russia's second-largest city due to the war in Ukraine and Western sanctions on Russia.

Key takeaways from the summit

One of the lingering questions in the various African summits held recently by some countries is whether partner summits add value to the search for a better African continent. That the summit held at all was a subtle message that life in Russia remains normal despite the Ukrainian war and the Western sanctions on the country. Though attended by 49 delegations, with only 17 heads of state participating at the summit compared with the 43 who attended the first summit in 2019, it must be underlined that not many people would feel comfortable visiting a country at war. Add to this the rumour that the US and other European countries mounted severe pressure on African leaders not to attend the summit, and the attendance would be seen as not too bad. Besides, some of the continent's most important leaders were there. They included Abdel Fattah el-Sisi of Egypt, Cyril Ramaphosa of South Africa, Macky Saul of Senegal, and Isaias Afwerki of Eritrea. Other prominent attendees included Moussa Faki Mahamat, Chairperson of the African Union Commission; Workneh Gebeyehu Negewo, Executive Secretary of the Intergovernmental Authority on Development (IGAD); Amina Salmane, Permanent Representative of the Arab Maghreb Union to the African Union; Dilma Rousseff, BRICS New Development Bank President; Benedict Oramah, President of the African Export-Import Bank (Afreximbank); and Gilberto Da Piedade Verissimo, President of the Economic Community of Central African States. Though the Nigerian President, Bola Ahmed Tinubu, was not there, he was represented by the country's Vice President, Kashim Shettima.

It is symbolic that the summit was attended by Yevgeny Prigozhin, the late founder and leader of the Russian private military contractor Wagner group. It was Prigozhin's first public appearance in Russia since launching an unsuccessful armed rebellion against the country's military hierarchy. Though private military companies (PMCs) are banned in Russia, Wagner has, since 2014 (when Russia annexed Crimea), emerged as one of Russia's most important foreign policy tools in several African countries (Rampe, 2023). Capitalising on anti-Western and anti-French sentiments, the Wagner group has bolstered its presence in several African countries, including the Central African Republic, Libya, Mali, Burkina Faso, Niger, and Sudan, and is looking for opportunities to extend its influence to other places.

The group has been operating in several African countries since 2017, often providing its clients with direct military support and related security services alongside propaganda efforts. It was estimated that in 2018, about 1000 Wagner mercenaries entered CAR to defend the government of President Faustin-Archange Touadéra against rebel attacks on the capital, Bangui. In return, Wagner subsidiaries received unrestricted logging rights and control of the lucrative Ndassima gold mine (Smith, 2023). The presence of Prigozhin at such a high-level summit indicated both tacit Russian support for Wagner's operations and Prigozhin's interest in exploring opportunities for further expansion in Africa.

The summit also provided an opportunity for Putin to make amends for his alleged shabby treatment of African leaders who had met with him to promote Africa's peace plan for the war in Ukraine. It should be recalled that on May 16, 2023, South Africa's president, Cyril Ramaphosa, announced new initiatives by African leaders for peace in Ukraine. In June 2023, the African peace mission, including representatives from South Africa, Egypt, Senegal, Congo-Brazzaville, Comoros, Zambia, and Uganda, visited both Ukraine and Russia to promote its peace deal. On June 17, 2023, Ramaphosa and his delegation met Russian President Vladimir Putin in St. Petersburg.

The delegation reportedly called on Putin to end the Russian, invasion of Ukraine but Putin was said to have rejected the peace plan because it was allegedly based on Russia accepting Ukraine's internationally recognised borders. Some have argued that Putin treated the African leaders with disdain and disrespect (Reuters, 2023). A South African professor, William Gumede, was for instance quoted as saying that the fact that Kyiv was bombed during the visit of the African peace mission to Ukraine was humiliating, "and then in Russia, Putin didn't even bother to listen to the delegation, basically interrupting them before they'd even finished speaking, implying there was no point in discussing anything as the war would continue." (Patta, 2023). Perhaps what was often left out by critics of Russia's treatment of the African delegation was that the time of the peace mission was probably inauspicious because Ukraine had just launched its much-anticipated counter-offensive to reclaim lost territories.

Be that as it may, the Second Summit was an opportunity for Putin to make amends, and Putin was mostly on charm offensive. Commenting on the African peace initiative, Putin was quoted as saying: "We did not reject them" but only maintained that "in order for this process to begin, there needs to be agreement on both sides" (Adler & Alsaafin,2023).

Alongside the war in Ukraine, food security was high on the agenda, especially following Russia's decision to withdraw from an international grain deal. The agreement brokered by the United Nations and Turkey in 2022 allowed the safe passage of agricultural goods through Ukraine's ports in the Black Sea. While most of the nearly 33 million metric tonnes exported since then did not reach the world's poorest countries, the deal was said to have helped reverse spiralling food prices by more than 20 percent, according to the UN (Duggal, 2023). Russia justified withdrawing from the grains deal by arguing that the conditions for extending the Black Sea Grain Initiative had been ignored. KorirSing'Oei, Kenya's principal secretary for foreign affairs, called Putin's decision to pull out of the deal "a stab in the back" (Radford & Armstrong, 2023).

As if in response to the charge of stabbing them in the back, Putin told African leaders that he would give them tens of thousands of tonnes of grain despite Western sanctions, which he claimed made it difficult for Moscow to export grain and fertilisers. He was quoted as saying that Russia was ready to replace Ukrainian grain exports to Africa on both a commercial and aid basis to fulfil what he said was Moscow's critical role in global food security. Russia said that Ukraine's failure to export more grain to poorer countries was one of the reasons it pulled out of the deal. Putin also complained that parts of the deal allowing for the export of Russian food and fertilisers had not been honoured (Wintour, 2023). On charges of insensitivity to millions of poor in the drought-hit horn of Africa, Putin was quoted as saying: "We will be ready to provide Burkina Faso, Zimbabwe, Mali, Somalia, the Central African Republic, and Eritrea with 25-50,000 metric tonnes of free grain each in the next three to four months" (Arise News, 2023).

The Summit also agreed to institutionalise Russo–Africa relations by establishing a Russia-Africa Partnership Forum to coordinate the development of the Russian-African relations. It designated the Russia–Africa Summit as its supreme body to be convened once every three years. It also proposed an annual political consultation between the Ministers of Foreign Affairs of the Russian Federation and African States.

The Summit equally re-stated its commitment to enthrone a multipolar world order. Putin hailed the "commitment of all our states to the formation of a just and democratic multipolar world order". The participants at the summit also signed a joint declaration that called for "the establishment of a more just, balanced, and stable multipolar world order, firmly opposing all types of international confrontation on the African continent." Putin promised that Russia would support African countries' efforts to "ensure compensation for colonial policies, including the restitution of cultural property displaced in the process of colonial plundering (France 24, 2023)."

Chapter Three

Russia's Renewed Interest in Africa

The Rise of Vladimir Putin in Russian Politics

After a period of relative isolationism following the implosion of the Soviet Union, Russia, which was the successor state to the USSR, began to re-assert itself on the global scene under Vladimir Putin.

Born in 1952, Putin studied law at Leningrad State University. He joined the KGB, the Soviet counterpart of the CIA, and was in the mid-1980s sent to the city of Dresden in East Germany. He returned to Leningrad in 1990 and claimed to have resigned from the KGB the following year. He felt deeply affected by the implosion of the Soviet Union, which he reportedly described as the "greatest geopolitical catastrophe" of the 20th century (NBC News, 2005). By 1998, Putin led the KGB's main successor organisation, and the following year, President Boris Yeltsin appointed him prime minister, the country's second-highest office. When an ailing and increasingly unpopular Yeltsin resigned on December 31, 1999, Putin took over as the acting president. Months later, he won the election to a full term. Under him, buoyed by rising oil and gas prices, Russia's economy improved in the early 2000s, and living standards rose. Putin was generally seen as bringing order to Russia after the tumultuous Yeltsin years, which were characterised by lawlessness, hyperinflation, and political instability.

Putin's Consolidation of Power and Relationship with the West

Largely because Russia's constitution barred a third consecutive term, Putin stepped down in 2008, with his long-time confidante Dmitry Medvedev taking over as president while he retained the role of prime minister but left no one in doubt about who was really in charge. When Medvedev's term ended in 2012, the two swapped positions and Putin again became president. He has occupied the top job ever since, at one point signing a law that would allow him to stay in power until 2036 (Reuters, 2021).

Many Western leaders initially approved of Putin, with U.S. President George W. Bush saying he had "looked the man in the eye," found him "very straightforward and trustworthy," and gotten a "sense of his soul." (Wyatt, 2001). Putin was the first foreign leader to call Bush following the terrorist attacks of September 11, 2001. Putin's relationship with the West, however, deteriorated partly over NATO's 2004 expansion into seven Eastern European countries and over pro-Western uprisings that broke out in Georgia and Ukraine. Furthermore, Putin was irked by U.S. lobbying to bring Georgia and Ukraine into NATO and by its support for an independent Kosovo (Bertrand, 2016).

In 2014, as tensions escalated over Ukraine, Russia was expelled from the Group of Eighth industrialised nations. He also infuriated the West by granting asylum to the US whistle-blower, Edward Snowden. He was also suspected of interfering in the 2016 US presidential election by greenlighting a computer hacking operation that infiltrated the campaign of Hilary Clinton (Abrams, 2019).

What does Russia Want from Africa?

As discussed in the previous chapter, the two Russo-Africa summits ended with the usual optics and photo-ops. The Sochi Summit spawned some $12.5 billion in business deals, largely in arms and grains, while the Second Summit seemed to be designed to prove to the world that despite the Russo-Ukraine war and the array of Western sanctions against the country, life remained pretty normal and safe in the country. But Putin's re-awakening interests in Africa, as could be seen from the two summits, also raises some interesting questions: what does Russia really want from Africa? How will Africa's traditional allies, especially the United States, respond to Russia's newfound love for the continent? And does Russia have what it takes to compete with China in Africa?

Russia seems to have many reasons for cosying up to Africa:

Goal 1: Projecting power on the global stage

Since African countries constitute the largest voting bloc in the United Nations, Russia probably figured out that the continent's support could be strategic in amplifying its positions in the United Nations and its agencies, especially the United Nations General Assembly, where decisions are taken by a two-thirds majority. In fact, in 2018, former U.S. National Security Adviser John Bolton accused Russia of selling arms to African countries in exchange for votes at the United Nations, among other nefarious motivations. According to Bolton, those votes helped to keep Africa's "strongmen in power, undermine peace and security, and run counter to the best interests of the African people". He was further quoted as saying that "the predatory practices pursued by China and Russia stunt economic growth in Africa; threaten the financial independence of African nations; inhibit opportunities for US investment; interfere with US military operations; and pose a significant threat to US national security interests" (Borger, 2018). Similarly, US Secretary of State Anthony Blinken accused Russia of exploiting conflict-hit and coup-vulnerable African countries in the Sahel region and said the United States was a better security partner for the continent than Russian military contractor Wagner (Asadu, 2024). In essence, it is obvious that the US and the West are taking a keen interest in Russia's re-awakened interest in Africa.

Goal 2: Accessing Africa's raw materials, natural resources, and investment opportunities

Economically, much of Russia's focus in Africa centres on energy. Several of Russia's investments in Africa are in the oil, gas, and nuclear power sectors. Russia probably reckons that 620 million people in Africa don't have electricity, which is an opportunity for the country to provide Russia's nuclear power industry with potential markets. Several Russian companies, such as Gazprom, Lukoil, Rostec and Rosatom, are active in Africa. Most of their activities are in Algeria, Angola, Egypt, Nigeria, and Uganda (Business & Human Rights Resources Centre, 2019). On April 13, 2023, Russia's Institute of Technological Development for the Fuel-Energy Complex organised a panel to discuss energy cooperation between Moscow and African countries. One of the experts, Gabriel Anicet Kotchofa, who served as the Republic of Benin's ambassador to Russia, was quoted as saying, "in Africa, we are waiting for Russia—for what Russia can do. I will tell you something that is never said today: we are tired of Europe" (Vernou, 2023).

In 2018, Great Dykes Investment (GDI), a joint venture between Russia's JSC Afromet and Zimbabwe's Pen East Ltd, announced plans to invest about 400 million dollars to build a precious metals mine and smelter in Zimbabwe. The company said the earmark is the first portion of a $3 billion investment for what it said would be its biggest platinum-group metals (PGM) asset. The joint venture was expected to produce up to 855,000 ounces (27 tonnes) of platinum group metals and gold per year from the Darwendale PGM project (Mining magazine, 2018). However, in 2022, Pen East Ltd announced that it had taken complete control of the venture because plans to raise $500 million by the end of 2020 and begin mining during 2021 did not materialise (Reuters, 2022). In November 2021, the Russian State Space Corporation "Roscosmos" signed a cooperation agreement with Zimbabwe to expand its satellite intelligence in the country to locate mineral deposits (Vernou, 2023).

In 2022, Russian Ambassador to Angola Vladimir Tararov announced plans to invest 1.2 billion U.S. dollars to build a fertiliser factory in Angola. The diplomat announced this at the end of a meeting with Fernando da Piedade Dias dos Santos, speaker of the Angolan Parliament. The diplomat reportedly said that Russia would finance studies for young Angolans who would be able to join the factory as engineers or technicians (Xinhua, 2022). In 2018, Alroser, a Russian mining company, increased its stake in the local producer Catoca to 41% in a $70 million deal that provides the diamond giant with a production base outside Russia. Despite joint ownership with Angola, Catoca operates under Russian management (Jamasmie, 2018).

In 2023, the Algerian Ministry of Industry said it had approved the construction of a vast carbon-free aluminium factory in partnership with Russia and dedicated to producing ecological green aluminium. The factory's annual production capacity is estimated at one million metric tonnes of aluminium, creating as many as 5,000 jobs. Furthermore, the same investor said it planned to build an integrated industrial complex comprising refineries and large factories (Nova News, 2023).

According to the Organisation for Economic Cooperation and Development, in 2020, Nigeria's export to Russia was put at $39.1 million, and the main products involved included cocoa beans, cocoa butter, and perfume plants. In the same period, Russia's exports to Nigeria amounted to $1.02 billion, and the products exported were mainly wheat, non-fillet frozen fish, and potassic fertilizers (Embassy of Nigeria in the Russian Federation, n.d.). During the Russia-Africa Summit in Sochi, both Nigeria and Russia put out a joint statement that there would be an agreement on a joint venture between the Nigerian National Petroleum Corporation (NNPC) and Russia's Lukoil focused on the refining sector in the West African country. Lukoil already operates in Nigeria, holding a stake in the deepwater oil block OML 140 offshore Nigeria. The statement also said that Nigeria and Russia agreed "to revive and solidify" the venture between the NNPC and Russia's Gazprom for gas infrastructure development in Nigeria (Gupte, Griffin & Bowles 2019). It will be recalled that in 2009, Gazprom and NNPC entered into a joint venture called Nigaz to invest in Nigeria's oil and gas infrastructure, but not much emerged from it. The two countries are now hoping to revive that partnership.

Russia's trade with Russia's trade with Egypt increased by 14 percent to a record $5.1 billion between January andNovember 2023, up from $4.5bn in 2022.

According to the figures, in the first 11 months of 2023, Egypt's exports to Russia were valued at $469 million, showing a decline of 13.7 per cent, compared to $543 million in 2022. During this period, Egypt's imports from Russia increased by 17.5% to $4.6 billion compared to the $3.9 billion recorded during the same period in 2022. Russian investments in Egypt in 2022/2023 increased by 117.6% to $141.2 million, compared to 2021/2022, when investments were valued at $64.9 million. It should be noted that the Russian firm, Rosatom, is building Egypt's first nuclear power plant in accordance with the Russian-Egyptian Intergovernmental Agreement of 2015. Under the deal, Rosatom is expected to build four power units with a total capacity of 4,800 megawatts (Egypt Today, 2024).

In Ethiopia, the Ethiopia-Russia Business Forum was held in Addis Ababa in December 2023 with the avowed objective of enhancing the economic and trade relations between the two countries. During the forum, Ethiopian officials reportedly briefed members of the Russian business community on the flourishing investment potentials and opportunities in the country. The Ethiopian officials reaffirmed the government's commitment to provide all the necessary support for the Russian companies interested in joining the Ethiopian market (Fana, 2023). Also, in March 2024, Russia sought to expand its influence in Ethiopia by signing an MoU that involved the construction of 2,000 health posts and the training of Ethiopian medical personnel. This initiative, which was undertaken by the Russian "Heroes" Charitable Foundation for Medical Staff Assistance, Ethiopian Bonga University, and the Russian Pan-African PPP Development Centre, was aimed at increasing access to primary healthcare in Ethiopia. The health posts to be built across Ethiopia were expected to focus on paramedical and obstetric centres, addressing critical areas such as midwifery and prenatal care (Volpi, 2024).

In South Africa, the country's national oil company, PetroSA, has chosen Russia's Gazprombank Africa as its preferred investment partner to restart its refinery at Mossel Bay. PetroSA officials were quoted as saying that they had taken legal advice and did not believe they would contravene Western sanctions should the Gazprombank deal to restart its gas-to-liquid (GTL) refinery proceed. The 45,000 barrel per day (bpd) Mossel Bay GTL plant has been under care and maintenance since 2020 because of dwindling domestic offshore gas resources (Roelf, 2023). In 2014, former President Jacob Zuma commissioned Russia's Rosatom energy company. If completed for £50 billion, the plants would have provided 23% of South Africa's energy (Pottinger, 2022).

Goal 3: Arms exports and security

Data by Stockholm International Peace Research Institute (SIPRI), a global arms trade tracker, show that between 2018 and 2022, Russia overtook China as the leading arms supplier to sub-Saharan African countries, with a market share of 26% compared to 21% over the previous period. Russia's market share rises considerably to 40% if the Maghreb is included because Algeria has historically been a major client of Russian arms companies. China, however, has seen its market share plummet from 29% to 18% in the sub-region, moving into second place, ahead of France (about 8%) and about 5% for the United States (Douet, 2023). A 2024 report for the European Parliament also noted that "Russia has concluded military cooperation agreements with 43 African countries and is a major, though declining, arms supplier to Africa" (Caprile & Pichon, 2024). The authors noted that the cooperation was not linked to democratic pledges and that in multiple African countries hit by coups, Russia continued or strengthened its military cooperation. Russia is, of course, the world's second-largest exporter of weaponry, after the United States, accounting for 20 per cent of global arms sales and $15 billion per year in revenue (Military Africa, 2023).

Russian arms are attractive to African leaders because, besides being relatively cheap, deals with Russia are not often held up by human rights concerns cited by other countries like France and the U.S. For instance, when the U.S. was dilly-dallying on selling arms to Nigeria to fight Boko Haram in 2014 on allegations of human rights abuses by Nigerian soldiers, Nigeria turned to Russia and was able to place an order for 12 Mi-35 attack helicopters. The order was placed in September 2015, and deliveries began in December 2016 (Defence Web, 2019).

Goal 4: Creating New Streams of Oil Supply

Russia also wants to use its mostly state-owned oil and gas companies to create new energy supply streams. In 2018, for instance, Nigerian oil and gas exploration company Oranto Petroleum said it would be cooperating with Russia's largest oil producer, Rosneft, to develop 21 oil assets across 17 African countries. At that time, Rosneft did not have any significant presence in Africa except for a 30-per cent stake in the giant Zohr gas field offshore Egypt in the Mediterranean and some prospects in Mozambique. It is thought that gaining access to more projects in Africa could be an important development for Rosneftin expanding its global footprint (Paraskova, 2018). As Pham (2014) noted:

> Russia is a major producer and exporter of oil and natural gas and does not need new supplies of energy from the continent. Under Putin, Russia has attempted to increase its control over energy sources throughout the world as a means of strengthening its own economic and political power and has shown interest in gaining control over the supply of oil and natural gas from Africa to European countries. For example, in 2006, following a visit by Putin to Algiers, the Russian natural gas giant Gazprom entered into an agreement with the Algerian state gas company, Sonatrach, to cooperate in exploration, extraction, and production of liquefied natural gas of Africa's second largest reserves. Just last month, Algeria invited Gazprom and Lukoil, Russia's second-largest oil company, to tender for the joint development of 30 fields that together make up one-fifth of the North African country. Combined, a Gazprom-Sonatrach partnership would control nearly 40 percent of Europe's gas consumption

In 2018, it was announced that the Nigerian oil and gas exploration company, Oranto Petroleum, would cooperate with Russia's largest oil producer, Rosneft, to develop 21 oil assets across Africa (Paraskova, 2018). In fact, several Russian companies have also made significant investments in Algeria's oil and gas industries and Libya, Nigeria, Ghana, Côte d'Ivoire, and Egypt.

Goal 5: Pursuit of a multipolar world

Putin has not left anyone in doubt that he is opposed to the current Western-dominated world system and seeks the creation of a multipolar world in which Russia will be the main or one of the main alternatives to the Western system. Putin uses the grouping of Brazil, Russia, India, China, and South Africa (BRICS), which was expanded in 2023 to include Ethiopia, Egypt, Iran, and the United Arab Emirates, to pursue this goal. Russia's influence in BRICS is enormous, and the inclusion of South Africa in this influential body can be viewed in the context of Russia endearing itself to the continent and through South Africa gaining more footing in Africa. At its 15th Summit held in Johannesburg on 22-24 August 2023, of the four countries admitted in the organisation's first expansion in 13 years, two—Ethiopia and Egypt—were African countries. The other two are Iran (which is at loggerheads with Western countries) and the United Arab Emirates. The inclusion of three African countries in the influential body, now known as BRICS+, could be seen in the context of Russia trying to endear itself to the continent. Putin also enthusiastically supports Africa's having at least a permanent seat at the UN Security Council (TRT Afrika, 2023), believing that if Africa were to achieve that goal, it would forever remain grateful to Russia for the support.

Goal 6: Cushioning the effects of Western sanctions

Russia's war with Ukraine, which began in February 2022, and the subsequent open confrontation with the West and the imposition of sanctions have put the spotlight on the African continent again as an area of geopolitical rivalry. Russia seeks to break the diplomatic and economic isolation imposed by the West and wants to re-assert its relevance as the new 'polycentric world' champion. It hopes to achieve this by combining its other goals on the continent, which were discussed above.

Like China, Russia likes to create a sense of comradeship with Africans by reminding them that they never colonised any part of Africa and that the country, in its relationship with Africa, emphasises collaboration over aid and, by implication, respects them more than the continent's traditional allies, who are often criticised for being patronising or condescending towards Africans and the continent. At the recent Russia-Africa Summit in Sochi, Vladimir Putin announced the writing off of $20 billion in debt owed by African countries and unveiled plans to double trade with African countries to $40 billion per annum.

Implications of Russia's deepening involvement in Africa

If Russia's renewed interest in Africa awakens America's waning interest in the continent, it could offer both threats and opportunities to the continent. There is, for instance, the possibility that Africa's traditional allies may try to undermine Russia's initiatives on the continent (and vice versa) as part of their geopolitical competition. Similarly, re-awakening the interest of Africa's traditional allies in the continent presents an opportunity for African countries to play the two powers against each other for their benefit—as they did during the Cold War. However, how far Russia succeeds with what it wants from Africa largely depends on the responses of Africa's traditional allies, especially the United States, to its deepening interest.

Chapter Four

Russo-Sino Relations in Africa

How Do Russia and China Compete in Africa?

Sino-Soviet Split

To discuss whether Russia and China compete in Africa and, if so, in what manner, one would first have to understand the Sino-Soviet split. Both countries were the leading socialist/communist countries during the Cold War. In 1956, then-Soviet leader Nikita Khrushchev denounced Joseph Vissarionovich Stalin, the Soviet revolutionary and politician who was the leader of the Soviet Union from 1924 until he died in 1953 and whose brand of socialism was often known as Stalinism, and consequently began what was called a de-Stalinisation of the Soviet Union. This led to a doctrinal disagreement between the two leading Communist countries on the application of Marxist-Leninist ideology. Mao Zedong, the founding father of Chinese socialism, viewed the Soviet Union's policies of de-Stalinisation and peaceful co-existence with the Western bloc as revisionism and a subtle critique of its belligerent stance toward the Western bloc.

Additionally, China was unhappy with the Soviet Union's growing ties with India, with which it had a border dispute. This was a territorial dispute over the ownership of two relatively large and smaller pieces of territory between China and India (Lüthi, 2008). As the doctrinal divergence between the two countries deepened, they also began to compete for the leadership of the Communist world, basically turning the bipolar world order of the Cold War days into a tri-polar world among the Peoples Republic of China, the Union of Soviet Socialist Republics, and the USA. Remarkably, Chairman Mao used the Sino-Soviet split to facilitate a rapprochement between China and the USA, which led to US President Richard Nixon visiting China in 1972. One of the consequences of this was the dilution of the notion of monolithic communism or the idea that communist countries were united by their socialist ideology. For instance, under Mao Zedong and Nikita Khrushchev, China and the USSR supported opposite factions in the civil wars in Zimbabwe, Angola, and Mozambique.

Over the last few decades since the collapse of Communism, fuelled by US trade rivalry with China, Beijing and Moscow seem to have taken on complementary roles and responsibilities in Africa, with China sticking to its principle of non-interference in the internal affairs of African countries and devoting itself primarily to economic diplomacy.

Subtle competition, overt cooperation in Africa

It can be argued that China and Russia compete and cooperate in Africa. With its vast natural resources, Africa has helped to fuel and sustain China's energy-intensive growth, leading to China becoming the largest bilateral trading partner of the continent since 2009 and a major source of construction investments. Also, as of April 2022, of the 54 African countries, 52 have already signed a BRI (Belt & Road Initiative) Memorandum of Understanding with China, indicating that the flagship project of Chinese foreign policy of the 21st century is penetrating the whole African continent (Gu, 2022).

In contrast to China, the dissolution of the USSR in 1991 led to 20 years of structural adjustment and a sort of isolationism for the country. However, as we noted earlier, under Putin, Russia began to project power again onto the global space, which included re-awakening its interest in Africa. Its focus on Africa seemed to be military cooperation, with the raging war against terrorism in parts of the continent giving Moscow an excuse to support African governments with the sale of armaments and other forms of military assistance. In the last two decades, for instance, Russia has managed to become the biggest arms exporter to Africa, accounting for 49% of total arms exports to Africa, according to the database of the Stockholm International Peace Research Institute (SIPRI). In 2018, five sub-Saharan African countries—Mali, Niger, Chad, Burkina Faso, and Mauritania—explicitly appealed to Moscow for support against Isis and al-Qaeda (ISPI, 2023). Over the past few years, trade between Russia and Africa has doubled, although it remains far below the value and volume of goods and services exchanged between Africa and China. As mentioned, Russian energy companies have significantly invested in the continent's oil and gas industries. Africa's non-alignment in the trade wars between China and the USA as well as the Russian-Ukraine war makes them 'beautiful brides' for Russia, China, and the West. Many African countries appear reluctant to join sanctions against Russia—just as they are opposed to Western paternalism and meddling in Africa's domestic affairs. Instead, they seem eager to exploit the economic isolation of Russia. Russia and China never failed to remind Africans that they did not take part in the slave trade and that they supported the liberation movements during the struggle for independence.

While for China, the continent seems to have lost some of its economic attractiveness due to the financial and security instability prevalent in many African countries, it also seems to have acquired greater importance for its political value. For instance, Africa is one of the areas of the world that has better received the Global Development Initiative, the Global Security Initiative, and the Global Civilisation Initiative, the three Chinese initiatives to promote Beijing's model of modernisation and global security governance abroad. It has been argued that Western sanctions against Russia are making it harder for Russia to sell its weapons to Africa, which in turn opens up the opportunity for Chinese-made arms, which already make up 22% of all arms sales to the continent—a mere two per cent points below Russia's shipments (ISPI, 2023).

A crucial question is whether the apparent cooperation between China and Russia in Africa would turn into an overt competition. One of the potential areas of mistrust is in the area of providing security for the continent. For instance, the Russian military company Wagner has been operating in many African countries since 2017, often providing its clients with direct military support in exchange for resource concessions and diplomatic support. Though China has never publicly complained about the activities of Wagner, there are fears that the activities of the mercenary group may pose a challenge to China on the continent, especially after some 'unknown gunmen' killed nine Chinese nationals in the Central African Republic, where Wagner and associated companies were given contracts to operate several mines (VOA, 2023).

Though the potential for conflict exists between Russia and China in Africa, both countries seem to have good grounds to manage any potential misunderstanding amicably for now. One of the reasons for this is that the continent provides both countries with the opportunity to articulate and advance their anti-Western grievances and to push for the 'democratisation of international relations' based on values of "equality and inclusiveness"–something that resonates well in most parts of Africa. South Africa dramatized the possibility of conflict and collaboration between China and Russia when it held a 10-day joint military drill with Russia and China along South Africa's east coast from February 17 to 27, 2023. Named Mosi (which means "smoke" in the local Tswana language), the exercises took place off the port cities of Durban and Richards Bay and involved more than 350 members of South Africa's armed forces serving alongside naval units of Russia and China. The event, which was held during the first anniversary of Russia's invasion of Ukraine, was seen by critics as a subtle endorsement of the Russian and Chinese narratives on the war. South Africa defended its decision to conduct joint military exercises with China and Russia by arguing that "South Africa, like any independent and sovereign state, has a right to conduct its foreign relations in line with its national interests" (cited in Ray, 2023).

Concerning the joint military exercise, Paul Nantulya, from the Africa Centre for Strategic Studies in Washington, was quoted as saying:

> China has a lot to gain from these exercises…. It is sending a very powerful signal to other African countries that in-person military training is now back on the table. ... China and [its] People's Liberation Army are basically back after years of closed borders during the pandemic (cited in Bartlett, 2023).

Nantulya was further quoted as saying:

> In terms of Russia, I think it's quite obvious that what China has been doing is trying to provide Russia some form of platform to be able to continue conducting international relations despite the fact that it's been heavily sanctioned (cited in Bartlett, 2023).

Bartlett quoted another expert, Priyal Singh, a senior researcher at the Institute for Security Studies (ISS) in Pretoria, as assessing the joint military exercises this way:

> This assists Beijing in illustrating to the West [and the world in general] that it has a foothold in the South Indian Ocean through its strong relations with South Africa. I believe this may be important to China, given the geopolitical

contestations being played out across the Indian Ocean region.

Remarkably, the military war game with South Africa took place amid heightened tensions between Washington and Beijing in the wake of the U.S. shooting down of an alleged Chinese spy balloon (Garamone, 2023). US Secretary of State Anthony Blinken had also alleged that China was considering supplying Russia with lethal weapons for its war against Ukraine, an allegation that China denied (Horti, 2023).

Chapter Five

Impact of the Ukraine War on Africa

While the devastating impacts of the Russo-Ukrainian war following Russia's invasion of Ukraine in February 2022 are well reported on, the secondary effect on Africa is less well understood—principally in economic terms but also strategically. More thinking is also needed into the possible global configuration of power after the war, where a contest over narratives will likely swing in favour of which of the two countries are perceived as emerging victorious. The key questions here are: What are the impacts of the war on the African continent? What are the likely drivers of the world order after the war? And what would Africa's responses be to these drivers?

Impact of Western Sanctions on Russia

Beginning with sanctions, western sanctions against Russia present both threats and opportunities for Africa. For instance, some African countries are sensing opportunities from the European Union's decision to phase out dependence on Russian oil and gas over three years and are positioning themselves to seize those opportunities. Countries in this category include Tanzania, where the country's President, Samia Suluhu Hassan, was quoted as saying that the conflict in Ukraine was generating growing interest from the European Union in the country's gas reserves, which are the sixth-largest in the continent (Resnick, 2022). Similarly, Senegal, which has oil and gas reserves of over 1 billion barrels located offshore between Senegal and Mauritania and where over 40 billion cubic feet of natural gas were discovered between 2014 and 2017 (SAIPEC, 2022), could also benefit from this. Again,

Nigeria, which is already a supplier of Liquefied Natural Gas to several European markets, could benefit. The Deputy Director-General of the European Commission's Department of Energy, Matthew Baldwin, who visited Abuja in July 2023, told journalists that the EU was looking to increase Liquified Natural Gas (LNG) imports from Nigeria to above the current levels (Okafor, 2023).

In July 2022, Algerian, Nigerien, and Nigerian Energy Ministers signed a Memorandum of Understanding (MoU) to construct a 4,000 gas pipeline across the Sahara Desert to supply Europe with additional gas. Under the arrangement, the Trans-Saharan Gas Pipeline (TSGP) would send billions of cubic meters of Nigerian gas to Algeria via Niger, and Algeria would then send it to European countries via the Transmed, which connects the country to Italy through Tunisia, and LNG (liquefied natural gas) transported by tankers. When the project was launched in 2009, the investment cost of the Trans-Saharan Gas Pipeline (TSGP) was estimated at 10 billion dollars. It was to span 4,128 km, of which 1,037 km are in Nigeria, 841 km in Niger, and 2,310 km in Algeria. The military coup in Niger in July 2023, however, seems to pose a big threat to the project (Aris, 2023).

African countries that produce natural resources that Russia also produces seem to have been witnessing an increase in demand due to the Western sanctions on Russia. For instance, South Africa, the world's second-largest producer of palladium after Russia, has reported a surge in the demand for the product, which is a critical input in automobiles and electronics. A South African mining analyst was quoted as saying:

> We produce half of the world's palladium and we produce 75% of the world's platinum and we produce about 90% of the world's rhodium... Because the world is restricting the platinum and palladium they get from Russia, it's squeezing the price up so we're in a great position (Stark, 2022).

Stark also noted that there has similarly been a surge in the demand for coal, of which South Africa is also a major producer. She was quoted as saying that before the Russo-Ukraine war, people would be lucky to get $100 per tonne of coal, but with the war, the prices shot up to as high as $300 per ton.

Other sanctions were imposed on Russia, such as the exclusion of seven Russian banks from SWIFT, the dominant messaging system underpinning global financial transactions, in March 2022 (but excluded those handling energy payments). Under the sanction regime announced by the EU, Russia's second-largest bank, VTB (VTBR.MM), Bank Otkritie, Novikombank, Promsvyazbank (PSKBI.MM), Bank Rossiya, Sovcombank, and VEB were each given ten days to wind down their SWIFT operations. Sberbank, Russia's largest lender, and Gazprombank were not included because they are the main channels for payments for Russian oil and gas, which EU countries still buy despite the conflict in Ukraine. On the basis for selecting the Russian banks that were targeted, an EU official was quoted as saying:

> All these banks that we have listed under SWIFT... they are all based on their connection to the state and the implicit connection to the war effort. We have not gone for a blanket ban across the whole banking system (Blenkinsop, 2022).

Similarly, in March 2022, Visa and Mastercard announced that they would suspend their network services in Russia. It should be recalled that major Western corporations across a range of industries halted their transactions in Russia since its invasion of Ukraine began on February 24, 2022, from US-based tech firms such as Intel and Airbnb to French luxury giants LVMH, Hermes, and Chanel. These moves by the West against Russia could potentially forewarn African countries that such measures could be visited on them if they have major policy or strategic differences with the West. One way African countries can show that they have learnt this lesson is not just in 'diversifying their dependencies' as most African countries seem to be currently doing but also in pushing for greater commitment to the Pan-African Payment and Settlement System (PAPSS), a cross-border, financial market infrastructure, launched by the African Import-Export Bank (Afrexim) to facilitate payment transactions across Africa without reliance on the US dollar and Western payment systems. In fact, on March 31 2022, the Board of Directors of Afreximbank approved the launch of a $4 billion Ukraine Crisis Adjustment Trade Financing Programme for Africa (UKAFPA), a programme of credit facilities that the Bank developed to manage the impacts of the Ukraine crisis on African economies and businesses (ECA, 2022). Greater commitment to PAPSSS would, in turn, help to facilitate the realisation of the integration goal of the African Union's African Continental Free Trade Area agreement, a pact connecting approximately 1.3 billion people across 54 countries with a combined GDP of $3.4 trillion. According to the World Bank, AfCFTA has the potential to increase African exports by $560 billion while boosting Africa's income by $450 billion by 2035 (Forum Friends of the African Continental Free Trade Area, 2024).

Despite the above potential gains from the Russo-Ukraine conflicts, the war also has some negative impacts. These include:

Disruption of Africa's recovery from COVID-19

Before the pandemic, many African economies were among the fastest growing globally, with improvements recorded in the Human Development Index. For instance, by the end of 2021, sub-Saharan Africa's growth rate of 4.5 per cent exceeded the projected growth rate of 3.7 per cent. According to the IMF's regional economic outlook for April 2022,

…that progress has been jeopardized by the Russian invasion of Ukraine which has triggered a global economic shock that is hitting the region at a time when countries' policy space to respond to it is minimal to nonexistent. Most notably, surging oil and food prices are straining the external and fiscal balances of commodity-importing countries and have increased food security concerns in the region. Moreover, the shock compounds some of the region's most pressing policy challenges, including the COVID-19 pandemic's social and economic legacy, climate change, heightened security risks in the Sahel, and the ongoing tightening of monetary policy in the United States. Because of this, the growth momentum for the region has weakened this year with economic activity expected to expand by 3.8 percent (IMF, 2022)

Essentially, the Russo-Ukraine war led to skyrocketing energy prices and high inflation in many Western countries, which has in turn led to imported inflation and, thus, the increased cost of living in several African countries. There have consequently been protracted protests against increasing hardship in several African countries. For instance, in August 2022, around 1000 workers marched to the Union buildings in Pretoria, South Africa's seat of government, calling on the government to contain rising prices and costs of living (Africa News, 2022). In early August 2023, labour unions across Nigeria protested against the soaring cost of living and said the 'palliative' measures announced by the country's President Bola Tinubu to ameliorate the hardships were not enough. In the capital of Abuja, protesters pulled down the gate of Nigeria's National Assembly before some lawmakers met with them and asked for more time to carry out their demands (Asadu, 2023). The protests have been episodic across many parts of the country since the Tinubu removed subsidy on premium spirits, otherwise known as fuel or petrol. In Nigeria, the annual inflation rate for August 2022 was 20.52%—the highest since 2005. Nigeria's inflation rate further rose to 33.69% in April

2024 compared to the March 2024 headline inflation rate, which was 33.20% (Channels TV, 2024).

Since then, prices of food and basic commodities have continued to soar to the sky as Nigerians continue to battle with the high cost of living and one of the country's toughest economic crises in living memory, sparked by the current government's twin policies of petrol subsidy removal and unification of forex windows. This culminated in the #EndBadGovernance protest, which began on August 1 and formally ended on August 10, 2024, where angry Nigerians across most parts of the country protested against the increasing hardship in the country, with some protesters in some Northern parts of the country calling for a military coup and waving the Russian flag.

In Ghana, hundreds of people took to the streets in the country's capital city of Accra on Saturday, September 23, as part of a three-day protest against worsening economic conditions and lack of accountability and mismanagement by the government in the West African country. Organised under the slogan #OccupyJulorbiHouse, the action had been called by a group known as Democracy Hub. There had been growing unrest, including by organised labour, as the country experienced what had been called "its worst economic crisis in a generation." The cost of living has remained high, with food prices rising by 122% in 2022. The same year, the Cedi lost 50% of its value against the US dollar. Fuel prices had reportedly soared by over 150% (Singh, 2023).

In Egypt, there have also been protests over rising costs of living. For instance, between January and March 2024, Amnesty International recorded at least four instances of arbitrary arrest and detention of individuals in three governorates in the country. Their 'sin' was that they complained about price hikes in comments on social media. In February 2024, authorities also questioned dozens of workers from a public sector company who participated in a strike demanding to be paid the minimum wage. Security forces also dispersed a demonstration in March 2024, where protesters blamed President Abdel Fattah al-Sisi for "starving" the poor, and arrested protesters (Hashash, 2024).

Russia's deals with several African countries could be under threat

Since 2015, Russia has signed over 20 bilateral military cooperation agreements with African countries. For instance, in the Central African Republic (CAR), President Faustin-Archange Touadéra even agreed to appoint a Russian citizen, Valeriy Zakharov, as his national security advisor. Russian interest in the resource-rich CAR has raised questions regarding its intentions in the violence-plagued nation where it has since January 2018 deployed 175 civilian experts and military instructors, mostly under the cover of a private security company, Sewa Security Services. It also delivered light weapons, such as pistols, artillery, and rocket launchers, and equally trained the CAR's army. According to the Stockholm International Peace Institute, by 2012-2016 Russia had become the largest supplier of arms to Africa, accounting for 35 per cent of arms exports to the region, followed by China (17 per cent), the United States (9.6 per cent), and France (6.9 per cent). As of 2018, it was estimated that exports of Russian-made weapons and military equipment to Africa amount to 4.6 billion USD annually, with a contract portfolio worth over 50 billion USD (Hedenskog, 2018). There are now fears that some of these deals may be in jeopardy, at least in the short to medium term, as Russia focuses on its military campaign in Ukraine.

Impact on food supply

The war has also affected the food supply in Africa, especially regarding wheat and sunflower products. It has been estimated that between 2018 and 2020, Africa imported from Russia

US$3.7 billion worth of wheat, or 32% of the continent's total wheat imports, and another US$1.4 billion or 12% of the continent's wheat imports, from Ukraine (The Conversation, 2022). Even before the war, food prices in several African countries were already at a ten-year high as a result of disruptions to food production and supply chains caused by or exacerbated by climate change, COVID-19, and crime, banditry, and terrorism, which prevented farmers from going to their farms in some countries. For instance, as of 2021, about 282 million people in Africa, or roughly 20 per cent of the population, were facing food insecurity and were undernourished— more than double the share in any other region of the world (Ulimwengu, 2023). The war in Ukraine has further escalated food prices, worsening the crisis of food insecurity.

Impact on cost of fertiliser

The war has equally affected the cost of fertiliser because the sanctions imposed on Russia (the world's largest exporter) have constrained its ability to export. Between 24 February 2022 and 3 March 2022, futures prices for urea fertiliser jumped by 32%, whilst diammonium phosphate (DAP) futures rose by 13% (Adibe, 2022). International fertiliser prices have eased but remain high by historical standards. For example, the price of urea reached a maximum of USD 925.00 per metric tonne in April 2022 and fell significantly to USD 443.75 per metric tonne in January 2023. Figure 5 shows the falling trend of fertiliser prices (in USD per metric tonne) from their peaks in 2022.

Fertilizer prices

$ per metric ton

— DAP — TSP — Urea — Potassium chloride

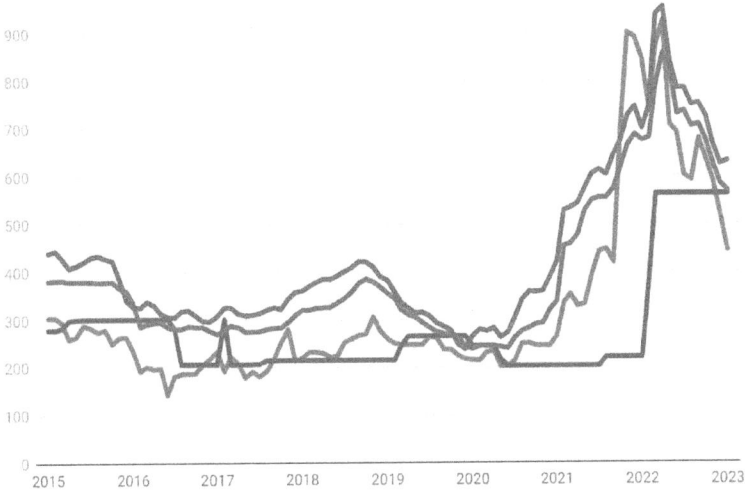

Chart: Joseph Glauber • Source: World Bank

Source: *Chopra (2023)*

One of the reasons for the decline in prices is also a decline in demand, as many farmers abandon or drastically reduce their use of fertilisers. Given the importance of fertiliser in agricultural production, there are concerns that a reduction in the use of fertilisers could lead to lower yields, which in turn could exacerbate the food insecurity facing the continent.

Impact on African students studying in Ukraine

The Russo-Ukrainian war also raised the issue of African students in Ukraine who fled the war. While some of those affected, especially medical students were offered places in countries like Grenada and Hungary, the war has left many with difficult choices, with some of the affected students facing the prospect of not qualifying at all. In Nigeria, for instance, many of the student returnees from Ukraine complained that, due to the war, their schools refused to release their transcripts or certificates to enable them to transfer to institutions in other locations (Okafor, 2022).

Impact on Russo-American competition in Africa

At a virtual Chatham House workshop in July 2021 entitled 'Russia's Quest for Global Influence—Africa', my presentation posed the question of whether Russia's increasing engagement with Africa could revive the Truman Doctrine—an American foreign policy strategy that made containing Soviet expansionism a priority for the United States. Announced by President Harry Truman on 12 March 1947, it led, in 1949, to the formation of the North Atlantic Treaty Organisaton (NATO). However, the war ends, with Sweden and Finland now full members of NATO and Switzerland announcing that in the wake of Russia's invasion of Ukraine, it would seek closer defence and security ties with the European Union and NATO (Saunders, 2023) while preserving its traditional neutrality, and with the West showing uncommon solidarity in their opposition to Russia's invasion of Ukraine, the distrust between both sides is likely to intensify. This could lead to what can best be called a 'neo-Cold War' order. However, unlike the Cold War, which was an ideological contest between capitalism/liberal democracy and socialism/communism, the projected neo-Cold War order (if it materialises) is likely to be driven by a contest between those supporting the current Western-dominated global configuration of power and those opposed to it—led by China, Russia, and others that traditionally hold grievances against the West.

In August 2022, the then-US House Speaker Nancy Pelosi defied warnings from Beijing and landed in a military aircraft in Taiwan. With the visit, Pelosi became the highest US official to arrive on the island for an official visit since 1997. Pelosi's visit was condemned by China, which saw it as a deliberate violation of its One China principle. It escalated the tension between China and the US, which could make a peaceful resolution of the Russo-Ukrainian war more difficult as it may push China into a bolder support of Russia in the war in the hope that Russia would in turn support it in its escalating tension with the US. Following the visit, Foreign Minister Wang Yi released a statement reiterating China's opposition to Ms Pelosi's visit and denounced it as "open political provocation", adding that it "seriously violates the One-China principle and harms China's sovereignty". He further said, "The US must stop obstructing China's great reunification. Taiwan is an inalienable part of China" (cited in Tan & Molloy, 2023). Shortly after the visit, the Chinese government, which views the island as part of the People's Republic of China and therefore considered Pelosi's visit provocative, announced a series of military drills. Though the United States has a long-standing relationship with Taiwan and is its main provider of military equipment, it maintains an official distance from the island to avoid angering China and provoking armed conflict.

Some opinions in Africa concurred that Pelosi's visit was indeed provocative. For instance, David Monyae, director of the Centre for Africa-China Studies at the University of Johannesburg, was quoted as saying that the visit by the speaker of the US House of Representatives showed that the US reneged on its promise to respect the One-China policy (Mlilo, 2022).

The crucial question is whether Pelosi's Taiwan visit and the critical opinions about it in Africa could push the continent into the side of Russia and China in a possible neo-Cold War order. With President Joe Biden promising that the USA would defend Taiwan militarily if China tries to annex it, and with China unlikely to give up its claim on the island, this could exacerbate the existing trade tension between China and the USA, with all its implications. For instance, it is feared that U.S. tariffs against China coupled with domestic and external pressures could slow down Chinese production, reducing in turn China's demand for raw materials from Africa. Of course, African countries could also benefit from the US-China rivalry if they can avoid a zero-sum game option when tapping into the rivalry between the two countries and if they can adopt measures that strategically play one power against the other while implementing long-term domestic policies that would help them maximise the benefits obtained from such a rivalry.

In many ways, the contest over narratives is likely to drive a projected neo-Cold War order after the Ukraine war has already begun. While the West justifies its support for Ukraine primarily on the need to protect Ukraine's sovereignty from alleged aggression by a bigger power, Russia blames it mainly on the West's eastward expansion of NATO. Russia questions the rationale for that expansion, especially given that its Cold War counterpart, the Warsaw Pact, was officially dissolved on July 1, 1991.

Africa after the Ukraine War

On May 18, 2022, I had an engaging interview with, as indicated earlier, (also known as Radio Liberty), a US Congress-funded news organisation founded in 1949 that focuses on Eastern Europe. It is remarkable that Radio Free Europe, founded at the early stages of the Cold War, remains active long after the Soviet Union unravelled, officially ending the Cold War era.

The interview was on Russia's role in Africa and how that role might likely be impacted by the war in Ukraine. Todd Prince, who contacted me for the interview, said he did so on the strength of my 2019 article for the Brookings Institution entitled 'What Does Russia Really Want From Africa?' Remarkably, on July 15, 2021, I had also taken part in a virtual workshop by London's Chatham House on Russia's Quest for Global Influence in Africa.

This reflection draws from the interview with Radio Free Europe, my contributions to the Chatham House workshop in July 2021, and my 2019 blog for Brookings Institution. The following are the takeaways:

The war will inevitably end one day

However long it lasts, the war will inevitably end one day, and most likely around a negotiating table—even if by accident it escalates into a Third World War. Its impact on Africa or Russia-Africa relations will largely depend on how the end of the war affects the current system polarity or distribution of power in the global system: if Ukraine is successfully turned to become Russia's version of America's Vietnam, it would contain Russia's resurgence as a world power under Putin and drive it to a new self-doubt akin to what happened after the collapse of the Soviet Union—at least for a while. It should be recalled that America's war in Vietnam was a protracted and divisive conflict that lasted for 20 years (1955-1975) and pitted the communist government of North Vietnam against South Vietnam, which was America's ally. It is estimated that more than 3 million people (including over 58,000 Americans) were killed in the war, with more than half of these being Vietnamese civilians (Hisory.com, 2024). Even after President Nixon signed the Paris Peace Accord in 1973, which ended the war and ordered the withdrawal of American troops from Vietnam the same year, the war continued to polarise Americans, leaving lasting effects on the country. Among other things, the war severely damaged the U.S. economy and weakened the morale of its military by its apparent inability to comprehensively defeat the less fancied Communist North Vietnam. In fact, the war effectively ended only when the Communist forces of North Vietnam seized control of South Vietnam in 1975 and unified the two Vietnams as the Socialist Republic of Vietnam the following year. The Vietnam War and its aftermath for a while forced the US into isolationism and weakened its commitment to internationalism.

A crucial question here is whether the aim of America's massive support for Ukraine in its war with Russia was to checkmate the latter's increasing projection of power onto the global system under Putin. If America succeeds in turning the Ukraine War into Russia's version of its own war in Vietnam, then we may likely see the country retreat from its pre-war attempts to resurge and project power onto the global system into the sort of self-doubt it had at the immediate end of the Cold War. If, on the other hand, it is seen as emerging victorious from the war, it will become more emboldened and will likely scout for other non-Western allies more aggressively in an attempt to create a new sphere of influence.

Will the end of the Ukraine War revive the Truman Doctrine?

At my presentation at the Chatham House workshop, I questioned whether Russia's deepening engagement with Africa could revive the Truman Doctrine. As discussed earlier, the Truman Doctrine is an American foreign policy that made containing Soviet expansion anywhere a priority for the United States. Announced by President Harry Truman on March 12, 1947, it led, in 1949, to the formation of the North Atlantic Treaty Organisation (NATO), an intergovernmental military alliance of 32 member states—30 European and 2 North American countries. The Truman Doctrine lasted until the implosion of the Soviet Union in 1991 and is often used to date the start of the Cold War. One of the criticisms of my Chatham House paper by some reviewers was my suggestion that US policy in Africa was influenced by Soviet expansionism in the continent. But if American foreign policy in Africa before the Ukrainian War was not overtly influenced by Soviet positions, as some argued, is the situation likely to change after the Ukraine War? However, once this war ends, the distrust between both sides is likely to intensify, leading to the possibility of what I call a "neo-Cold War order" (Adibe, 2022). However, unlike the old Cold War, which was fought based on an ideological contest between capitalism/liberal democracy and socialism/communism, the neo-Cold War order is likely to be driven by a contest between those supporting the current Western-dominated global configuration of power and those opposed to it, led by China, Russia and others that traditionally hold grouses against the West. With President Joe Biden promising that the USA would defend Taiwan militarily if China attached it (Brunnstrom & Hunnicutt, 2023) and China unlikely to give up its claim on the island, a closer collaboration between China and Russia, after the war seems likely—in the classic case of the enemy of my enemy is my friend. The character of the neo-Cold War order will largely depend on which side emerges stronger from the Ukrainian conflict.

In many ways, the contest over narratives and moral high grounds, which is likely to drive the neo-Cold War order after the Ukraine war, has already begun: while the West justifies its support for Ukraine on the need to protect Ukraine's sovereignty from alleged aggression by a bigger power, Russia blames it on the West's Eastward expansion of NATO, an organisation set up in 1949 by the United States, Canada, and several Western European nations to provide collective security against the defunct Soviet Union. Russia further questions the rationale for that expansion, especially given that its Cold War counterpart, the Warsaw Pact, was officially dissolved on July 1, 1991.

Russia's justifications for its military operations in Ukraine seem to resonate well with some Africans. For instance, on March 2, 2022, 17 African countries abstained from a United Nations vote condemning Russia's invasion of Ukraine, representing almost half of all countries that sat on the fence (Mureithi, 2022). In the same vein, on April 7, 2022, Nigeria, alongside 21 other African countries, abstained from voting to suspend Russia from the UN Human Rights Council over its invasion of Ukraine in an apparent disagreement with the 93 members of the Council, which voted in favour of the suspension (Jones, 2022).

Refugees to Africa from the West?

A question many analysts have shied away from asking is, whether Africa is sufficiently positioned to absorb refugees from the West in the event of the Ukrainian war escalating into World War III. Though this possibility seems remote and undesirable, it will not be out of place for Africa to engage in scenario mappings that will include this option.

Chapter Six

Wagner in Africa: An Appraisal

The growth of the Wagner Group in Africa

The chapter reflects on the Wagner Group, a private military company (PMC), which has in recent years become one of Russia's most influential foreign policy tools. Founded by Dmitry Utkin, a retired veteran of Russia's intelligence agency, the GRU, it was bankrolled by Yevgeny Prigozhin, better known as "Putin's cook" (or chef). The group came to prominence in 2014 during Russia's annexation of Crimea. Prigozhin, who was very closely associated with the group, had a shady past, having been sentenced in 1981 to thirteen years' imprisonment in a medium-security penal colony for robbery, theft, fraud, and involving minors in criminal activity (Meduza, 2021). Prigozhin later turned into an entrepreneur, establishing a string of highly regarded restaurants in Saint Petersburg through which he met and established a relationship with Putin, who was at that time active in municipal politics. The relationship between the two blossomed, with Prigozhin becoming Putin's trusted and intimate confidant. Dubbed "Putin's chef," Prigozhin moved from the actual catering business into the private military company (PMC) business. The Wagner Group has operated in as many as 28 countries across the globe, including in Eastern Europe (i.e., Ukraine), the Middle East (i.e., Syria), and South America (i.e., Venezuela). It has become most visible on the African continent, having deployed to at least 18 African states since 2016 (Faulkner, 2022:30). Despite the legal prohibition of private military companies in Russia, Wagner operated unmolested with implicit endorsement and even suspected funding from the Russian government. In fact, Putin, while declaring an investigation into Wagner Group spending on 27 June 2023, claimed that the Russian state fully funded Wagner from the country's defence budget and state budget and that from May 2022 to May 2023 alone, the Russian state paid 86.262 billion RUB to the group, approximately $1 billion (Nanu, 2023).

Wagner is not a single entity but rather a complex network of businesses and mercenary groups whose operations have been closely tied to the Russian military and intelligence community. Estimates of the number of its soldiers in Africa vary widely from between 1,500 and 2000 (Hammer, 2024) to 5000 (Rampe, 2023) and are mostly made up of a combination of former Russian soldiers, convicts, and foreign nationals. In January 2023, the U.S. government designated Wagner as a significant transnational criminal organisation. This essentially means that the United States, under Executive Order 13581 established in 2011, considers the Wagner Group as posing "an unusual and extraordinary threat to the national security, foreign policy, and economy of the United States."

The Wagner Group has established operations in several African countries since 2017, where it often provides security services and paramilitary assistance for troubled regimes in exchange for resource concessions and diplomatic support. Wagner's presence in Africa is particularly felt in the Central African Republic (CAR), Libya, Mali, Sudan, Burkina Faso, and Niger, all of which have problematic relationships with the West, particularly France, due to colonial legacies and inherent political and philosophical differences.

Its services vary based on the needs of its clients – which include both governments and rebel groups. For this reason, it has as its clients both African governments in combat operations against rebel groups in their countries and vice versa. A good example is the Central African Republic, where approximately one thousand Wagner soldiers fought to defend the government of President

Faustin-Archange Touadéra against rebel attacks on the capital, Bangui. In return, Wagner's subsidiaries were said to have been granted unrestricted logging rights and control of the lucrative Ndassima gold mine (Felbab-Brown, 2023). In the same vein, in 2019, Wagner fighters were deployed to Mozambique to help fight the self-proclaimed Islamic State in the northern Cabo Delgado province (ACLED, 2023). However, the group failed to contain the insurgency and withdrew from the area after a few months.

In 2017, the Wagner Group deployed some 500 men to put down local uprisings against the government of Sudan's dictator Omar al-Bashir in exchange for exclusive gold mining rights in the country (Fasanotti, 2022). Wagner's support is augmented by official Russian military assistance, such as in Mali, where the armed forces were said to have received combat and surveillance aircraft from Moscow (Rampe, 2023). Patel (2022) argued that Wagner Group's disinformation and propaganda ecosystem works to amplify pro-Russia narratives to curry favour with African audiences and drum up support for Wagner Group services across Africa. He also contends that Wagner's involvement in Africa has exacerbated rather than attenuated regional insecurity and that the Group is equally guilty of human rights violations. Critics have also argued that the status of Wagner as PMC limits the financial costs of Russian interventions abroad while giving Russia plausible deniability (Rampe, 2023).

Prigozhin's rebellion and death

In the course of the Russo-Ukrainian war, Prigozhin became very critical of Russia's Minister of Defence Sergei Shoigu and Chief of the General Staff Valery Gerasimov. He publicly blamed these two for Russia's initial setbacks during the Wagner-led Battle of Bakhmut. As the antipathy between Prigozhin and the commanders of the Russian army hardened, on 23 June 2023, Prigozhin led the Wagner group in a major uprising against the government of Russia. He called the uprising a "march for justice" against the Russian military establishment and demanded that Shoigu and Gerasimov be removed from their positions. He also declared that Russia's official justification for attacking Ukraine was a lie (Sauer, 2023). In a televised address, President Putin denounced the Wagner Group's actions as treason and vowed to quell the uprising.

The Wagner fighters first captured Rostov-on-Don, the headquarters of Russia's Southern Military District, while their armoured column advanced towards the country's capital, Moscow. However, before the Wagner fighters could reach Moscow, the President of Belarus, Alexander Lukashenko, brokered a peace deal with Prigozhin, who subsequently agreed to end the rebellion. The Wagner troops abandoned their push to Moscow on the evening of 24 June. Following the peace deal, Russia's Federal Security Services, which had vowed to prosecute the Wagner Group for armed rebellion against the Russian state under Article 279 of the country's Criminal Code, dropped all charges against Prigozhin and his Wagner Group on 27 June 2023. On 23 August 2023, exactly two months after the rebellion started, Prigozhin was killed in a plane crash alongside other senior Wagner officials.

Wagner after Yevgeny Prigozhin

The elimination of Prigozhin raised some interesting questions: What would be the impact of his death on Wagner's operations in Africa and the Middle East? Will his death create a power vacuum? Will the group become stronger or weaker? Does Russia's Ministry of Defence, or others from the security apparatus, have the means to take over Wagner's activities while the war in Ukraine rages? What would be the impact of his death on Russo-Africa relations?

In fact, following the mutiny by Wagner fighters, when Prigozhin was reported to have said he would move to

Belarus (before he died in a plane crash), Russian Foreign Minister Sergei Lavrov quickly assured that the events "will not affect the relationship between Moscow and its African friends" (Armstrong, 2023). Some have argued that Russia is so heavily dependent on Wagner's assets abroad and that the unwinding of the group's operations in Africa would cause a rapid contraction of Russia's influence in the continent (Siegle, 2023). So far, it would seem that Russia's appeal as a security guarantor and alternative to both the West and China (which does not really get involved militarily in Africa) remains unaffected by the death of Prigozhin. This could be seen from the #EndBadGovernance protest across the country from August 1-10, 2024, in which several protesters, especially in the northern part of the country, were seen waving the Russian flag. We also saw it in the increased relationship between Wagner Group and Burkina Faso, Mali, and Niger, where the French authorities were asked to leave after the military coups in these countries and their departure from the Economic Community of West African States.

One of the possible reasons for this is that Russia's provision of regime survival packages for countries under its sphere of influence supersedes any other potential gains from its traditional Western allies. Essentially because of Russia's reputation as a security guarantor for its African partners using Wagner (who often do not distinguish between the PMC and the Russian state), even if a new structure emerges to replace the structure of the WAGNER headed by Prigozhin, it is unlikely to fundamentally alter Moscow's current position on the continent. In fact, a Polish think-tank, the Polish Institute of International Affairs (PISM), claimed to have observed that in the wake of Prigozhin's death, "the Russian state's attention in [Africa] not only did not weaken but strengthened"(cited in Murphy, 2024). The report by Murphy further claimed that the BBC obtained documents that showed that Russia was offering "regime survival packages" to African countries in exchange for access to strategically important natural resources—an approach previously favoured by the Wagner Group. He equally claimed that the plan is being offered by a so-called Russian 'expeditionary group' nicknamed Africa Corps and commanded by former GRU Gen. Andrey Averyanov, who previously oversaw secretive operations specialising in targeting, killings, and destabilising foreign governments. He further claimed in the BBC report that the Africa Corps has effectively replaced Wagner in West Africa and that it is only in the Central African Republic (CAR) that Wagner still operates in any shadow of its former shape, allegedly controlled by Prigozhin's son Pavel (Murphy, 2024).

Chapter Seven

Conclusions, Highlights, and Recommendations

Conclusions

The study discusses my academic journey in International Relations using the prism of Russo-Africa relations. It does this from a historical perspective with a particular focus on what Russia wants from Africa. It briefly discussed the historical relationship between Russia (later Soviet Union) and some African countries—Egypt, Ethiopia, South Africa and Nigeria.

The study relied mostly on secondary sources of information to gather materials—books, journals, internet blogs, and newspaper articles. For analysis, it relied on content analysis of the gathered materials and the use of deductive and inductive reasoning to arrive at its conclusions. The analyses were carried out within the theoretical frame of the Truman Doctrine—a doctrine enunciated by President Harry Truman in 1947 that made it obligatory for the US to contain Soviet expansionism anywhere. Historians often date the beginning of the Cold War to 1947, when the Truman Doctrine was enunciated.

The study traced the early contacts between Russia and African countries to as far back as the late 18th century, when the Russian Empire sought support from the rulers of Morocco, Egypt, and Tunisia in its confrontation with the Ottoman Empire. It noted that Russo-Africa relations became low-keyed shortly after the October Revolution of 1917 in Russia, which enthroned communism as the official state ideology—even though the socialist revolution in that country appeared to have inspired some socialist groups in Africa. During the colonial struggle for independence and as socialism became consolidated in the Soviet Union, a theoretical connection was established between the anti-colonial struggles on the continent and imperialism. In fact, Vladimir Lenin, the founder of Soviet communism, argued in his book, *Imperialism: The Highest Stage of Capitalism* (1917) that imperialism was driven by the quest for capital accumulation. By doing so, he was able to establish a theoretical link between the anti-colonial struggles in the colonies and the struggles against capitalism in the Soviet Union. This provided a theoretical basis for the Soviet support of many of the anti-colonial movements in Africa at that time.

The study also discussed the two Russo-Africa summits. It noted that the first Russo-Africa summit was held in Sochi, Russia, from October 23–25 2019 and that during that summit, Russia welcomed 43 African heads of state or government, along with dozens of business and community leaders. It also noted that the summit ended with the usual optics and spawned $12.5 billion in business deals, largely in arms and grains. The study equally discussed the Second Russo-Africa Summit, which was originally scheduled to be held at the African Union headquarters in Addis Ababa, Ethiopia, in October 2022, but was eventually held at the Expo Forum in St. Petersburg, Russia's second-largest city after Moscow, on July 27 and 28 of 2023. It argued that the fact that the summit was held at all was a subtle message that life in Russia remained normal despite the Ukrainian war and the Western sanctions on the country. Though only 17 heads of state participated at the Second Summit compared with the 43 who attended the first summit in 2019, the study argued that given the war situation in the country and the apparent pressure from Africa's traditional allies not to attend the summit, the Second Summit could not be called a failure. Among other things, the study argued that the Second Summit provided an opportunity for President Putin to make amends for his alleged shabby treatment of African leaders who had met with him in June 2023 to promote Africa's peace plan for the war in Ukraine. The African delegation reportedly called on Putin to end the Russian invasion of Ukraine, but Putin was said to have rejected the peace plan because it was allegedly based on Russia accepting Ukraine's internationally recognised borders.

The study equally discussed Russia's renewed interest in Africa since the emergence of Putin as Russia's President, starting on December 31, 1999, when he took over as the acting president of the country from the increasingly ailing Boris Yeltsin. It noted that under Putin, Russia began to re-assert itself and project power onto the global stage. It also quickly emerged as the largest supplier of arms to Africa. The study discussed Russia's main interest in Africa during this period.

It also analysed how China and Russia not only compete subtly in Africa but also cooperate. It discussed Sino-Russo relations in the context of the Sino-Soviet split of 1956, when the Russian leader Nikita Khrushchev denounced Joseph Vissarionovich Stalin, the Soviet revolutionary and politician who was the leader of the Soviet Union from 1924 until he died in 1953, and consequently began what was called a de-Stalinisation of the Soviet Union. With both countries interested in a new world order that is not dominated by the Western system and both having issues with the USA, the study contended that the two countries have a shared interest, if not in dismantling the Western-dominated system, then at least in creating a multipolar world in which they will also be critical players. Following this, the study noted that the competition between the two countries is subtle but never openly antagonistic— following the aphorism that the enemy of my enemy is my friend.

We equally discussed the impact of the Ukraine war on Africa. We discussed the impact of Western sanctions on Russia following its war with Ukraine, noting the opportunities and threats they threw up for the continent. For instance, we noted that while the sanctions have led to an upsurge in the demand for some raw materials produced by some African countries, the war also had negative impacts, such as its disruption of Africa's recovery from COVID-19, the threat posed to Russia's deals with several African countries as it re-redirected resources to the war in Ukraine, and the war's negative impacts on food supplies, such as wheat and fertiliser, etc. We did a bit of future studies by projecting what would be the likely configuration of global power after the Ukraine war and how such would affect Africa.

In the last section of the work, the study focused on the Private Military Company (PMC), Wagner Group, in Africa. It noted that the Wagner Group has established operations in several African countries since 2017, where it often provides security and paramilitary services for troubled regimes in exchange for resource concessions and diplomatic support. It noted that Wagner's presence in Africa is particularly felt in the Central African Republic (CAR), Libya, Mali, Sudan, Burkina Faso, and Niger, all of which have problematic relationships with the West, particularly France, due to colonial legacies and inherent political and philosophical differences. The study equally reflected on the fate of the Wagner group after the death of Prigozhin. It noted that it seems that there is a consensus that Russia is so heavily dependent on the Wagner's assets abroad that the unwinding of the group's operations in the continent would cause a rapid contraction of her influence there. Following from this and the fact that many of its clients in Africa often do not distinguish between the PMC and the Russian State, which they see as providing good regime survival packages, the study contends that Prigozhin's death is unlikely to diminish Russia's interest in Africa.

Summary of the Highlights and Recommendations

The following are the key highlights from the study:

1. Russia's relations with Africa date as far back as the late 18th century, when the Russian Empire sought support from the rulers of Morocco, Egypt, and Tunisia in its confrontation with the Ottoman Empire. This

2. relationship blossomed during the independence struggle by African countries but relapsed after the implosion of the Soviet Union in 1991, when the country, apparently engulfed in an identity crisis, went into isolation. Russia's renewed interest in Africa is part of its attempts to project power onto the global stage under Putin to create a multipolar world.

3. In its renewed interest in Africa, Russia wants access to Africa's raw materials and natural resources, markets for its armaments, Africa's support in the United Nations and its agencies, and the creation of new streams of oil supply. Since the Russo-Ukraine War and the resulting Western sanctions, Russia also needs Africa to help cushion the effects of the sanctions.

4. The Russo-Ukraine War has not only disrupted Africa's recovery from the COVID-19 pandemic but also poses a threat to some deals signed between Russia and several African countries. The war also has implications for the food supply on the continent.

5. Russia has built a reputation in Africa not just as an alternative to the West but also as a security guarantor for its African partners using the PMC, Wagner.

Key recommendations

1. Africa should not see Russia's renewed interest in the continent as an opportunity to diversify its dependency but rather as a chance to pursue truly non-aligned and sustainable policies that will benefit its people.

2. The threats from the Russo-Ukraine war also embed opportunities for the continent. For example, it presents an opportunity for the continent to look more inward in

developing its agriculture and food supply chains.

3. The Western sanctions against Russia in which Western payment systems like Visa and Mastercard announced a suspension of their network services in Russia should warn African leaders that such fate could befall them if they fall out of line. This should ideally make them more committed to the Pan-African Payment and Settlement System (PAPSS) a cross-border financial market infrastructure launched by the African Import-Export Bank (Afrexim) to facilitate payment transactions across Africa without reliance on the US dollar and the Western payment systems. It should equally push them towards greater commitment to the African Continental Free Trade Area (AfCFTA) established in 2018 to boost intra-African trade.

4. Regarding the impact of the Russo-Ukraine War on Africa, a question many analysts have shied away from asking is, whether Africa is sufficiently positioned to absorb refugees from the West in the event of the Ukrainian war escalating into World War III. Though this possibility seems remote and undesirable, it will not be out of place for Africa to engage in scenario mappings that will include this option.

5. Russia's provision of regime survival packages for countries under its sphere of influence (which some African states seem to prioritise over potential gains from their traditional Western allies) means that even if a new structure emerges to replace the structure of the WAGNER headed by the late Prigozhin, it is unlikely to fundamentally alter Moscow's current position on the continent. This means being creative on how to benefit from the competition between the big powers on the continent.

Postscript

Trump's election as the 47th President of the USA and the Trajectory of the Russo-Ukraine War

The November 5, 2024 Presidential election in the USA has come and gone. Americans have spoken. Donald Trump is returning to the White House as the country's 47th President with a convincing win, poling 312 electoral votes to Kamala Harris' 226. A crucial question is how would Trump's election affect the trajectory of Russo-Ukraine War? And how would this in turn affect Africa?

The general assumption is that Trump would pursue a somewhat isolationist policy within the framework of his campaign slogan of Make America Great Again (MAGA) and that he would more likely pull all the funding for Ukraine. During the campaign, Trump had derisively called Ukraine's President Volodymyr Zelensky, the greatest salesman in history (Dorn, 2024), implying that he had through sheer marketing skills got more than he deserved from the US and other NATO members who had been supporting his war efforts. Trump had also suggested that he could impose a blanket 20% tariff on all goods imported into the U.S., with a tariff of up to 60% for Chinese products and one as high as 2,000% on vehicles built in Mexico (Wiseman, 2024). For the European Union, meanwhile, Trump has said the 27-nation bloc will pay a "big price" for not buying enough American exports (Reuters, 2024).

Zelensky himself reinforced this belief that the second coming of Trump might be bad news for Ukraine when, after a telephone conversation with Trump following the latter's electoral victory over Kamala Harris, he told his countrymen and women that he was certain that the war with Russia would "end sooner" than it would have been once Donald Trump is sworn in as the President of the United States in January 2025.

It is certain that the war will end sooner with the policies of the team that will now lead the White House. This is their approach, their promise to their citizens," he was reported to have said in an interview with the Ukrainian media outlet, Suspilne. He added that Ukraine "must do everything so that this war ends next year, ends through diplomatic means (Arise News, 2024).

It should be noted that the US has been the biggest arms supplier to Ukraine in the course of the war. For instance, between February 2022 when the war began to the end of June 2024, it delivered or committed to deliver weapons and equipment worth $55.5bn (£41.5bn), according to the German research organization, Kiel Institute for the World Economy (cited in Adibe, 2024). At present (i.e November 19, 2024) the momentum in the war seems to be with the Russians. For instance, Russia is reportedly winning significant swathes of territory in eastern Ukraine. Russia's recent seizure of the strategically important city of Vuhledar appears to have cleared the way for possible Moscow's advances deeper into Ukraine. It is also reported that Moscow is preparing for an offensive using about 10,000 North Korean soldiers and about 40,000 Russians in the Kursk region of Russia, where Ukrainian forces have been struggling to defend the territory they captured during the summer (Brennan, 2024) With this picture in mind, it is understandable why there are apprehensions among Ukrainians and their supporters in the war. The thinking appears to be that the country should use the remaining part of the supportive Biden presidency to do whatever they can to push back the Russians and strengthen their bargaining position before Trump becomes the substantive President in January 2025 and forces them into a negotiating table. Recently, it was announced that the Biden administration has allowed Ukraine to use long-range American missiles against targets in Russia (Stone & Pamuk, 2024) in a move that would mark a new round of tension in the war.

There is no doubt that Trump would like to reduce or drastically cut funding to Ukraine in keeping with his campaign promise of America First. There are however other considerations that might influence his decisions on the Ukraine war: The first is that Trump, who regards himself as the ultimate dealmaker, is a very transactional politician – and might be open to be influenced by Ukraine or the Europeans depending on the sort of 'deal' he is offered. The German Chancellor Olaf Scholz, who spoke with Trump after the US election, alluded to this when he reportedly told the German media that the incoming US leader had a "more nuanced" position on the war than was commonly assumed (Barigazzi, 2024). It has been suggested that Zelensky could offer two 'deals' to Trump: The first will be for Ukrainian troops to replace some American units in Europe after the war in order to reduce the cost of America's commitment to NATO. The second could be opening up some of Ukraine's resources to the US and other western allies. Offers such as these would however be contingent upon Ukraine winning the war and being admitted into NATO - which at present is far from certain.

The second consideration for Trump is geopolitical and geo strategic. South Korea, an American ally, has reportedly supplied hundreds of thousands of artillery shells to Ukraine via the United States and had also pledged a $2.3bn low-interest loan to Kyiv (Mirovalev, 2024). South Korea is the world's 10th-largest arms exporter and its clients already include four nations that border Russia – Poland, Estonia, Finland and Norway. The South Korean systems are meant to supplement Patriots, the advanced American air defence systems. It is said that the South Korean laser needs nothing but electricity – and could be deployed to the Ukrainian cities that have no Patriots or similar Western or Taiwanese air defence systems. A crucial question is whether Trump would be insensitive to deals entered with Kiev by its ally South Korea in his decision on how he wants the Ukrainian war to end or even in any decision to stop funding Ukraine's war efforts.

Related to the above is the report that around 10,000 North Koreans, USA's historical enemy, has joined the war on the Russian side, with the possibility of Belarus also joining. Following the axiom that the friend to my enemy is my enemy or at least not to be trusted, the increasing collaboration between North Korea and Russia is also a factor to be taken into consideration by Trump in his decision on the Russo-Ukraine war. Similarly, claims by Ukraine's Western allies in September 2024 that Iran, another enemy of the West, has sent short-range ballistic missiles to Russia in a major escalation (Euronews, 2024), – a claim Tehran has rejected as completely baseless and false - will be another consideration.

A third major consideration that could influence Trump's decision is the Truman Doctrine that makes it an article of faith during the Cold War for the US to seek to contain Soviet expansionism. There have been signs of America's revival of the Truman Doctrine since the Putin presidency, especially after Russia's annexation of the Crimea in 2014. Russia has not hidden its desire to create a multipolar world in a bid to overthrow or whittle down the influence of the current Western dominated security and governance systems around the world. Irrespective of the nature of the personal relationship between Putin and Trump, it is unlikely that Trump would not respond to a resurgent Russia's attempt to whittle down its global influence.

As a dealmaker, Trump is likely to be looking for a deal which would reduce the US military presence in Europe, drastically cut the military assistance to Ukraine, and give Kiev a long term hope of joining NATO in exchange for territorial concessions to Russia. In this way, Trump would be able to publicly claim that he won the peace without undermining NATO and without making Russia appear the outright winner in any diplomatic negotiations to end the war.

However the war ends, it will be a mixed bag for the world and Africa globally. For instance African countries that benefit from the current Western sanctions against Russia would have to re-adjust if Western sanctions are eased while those that have been hurt by the sanctions, especially importers of wheat and fertilizers from Russia and Ukraine, may heave a sigh of relief.

References

Abrams, Abigail (2019, April 18). Here's what we know so far about Russia's 2016 meddling. *Time magazine*. https://time.com/5565991/russia-influence-2016-election/

ACLED (2023, August 2). Moving out of the shadows: shifts in Wagner Group operations around the world. https://acleddata.com/2023/08/02/moving-out-of-the-shadows-shifts-in-wagner-group-operations-around-the-world/

Adem, Seifudein, Adibe, Jideofor & Bangura, Abdul Karim (2016, eds.). *A Giant Tree has Fallen: Tributes to Ali Al-Amin Mazrui*. African Books Collective.

Adetokunbo, Abiodun. (2017). Nigeria-Russia bilateral relations: problems and prospects. *RUDN Journal of Russian History*. Vol. 16 No 3, P. 480

Adibe, Jideofor (2024, November 19). The Russo-Ukraine war and the second coming of Donald Trump. Vanguard. https://www.vanguardngr.com/2024/11/the-russo-ukraine-war-and-the-second-coming-of-donald-trump-by-jideofor-adibe/

Adibe, Jideofor. (2022, December 20). The Russo-Ukrainian war's impact: Africa and a 'Neo-Cold War', *E-International Relations*. https://www.e-ir.info/2022/12/20/the-russo-ukrainian-wars-impact-africa-and-a-neo-cold-war/#:~:text=Between%2024%20February%202022%20and,food%20insecurity%20facing%20the%20continent.

Adibe, Jideofor. (2019, November 14). What does Russia really want from Africa? *Brookings Institution*. https://www.brookings.edu/articles/what-does-russia-really-want-from-africa/

Adibe, Jideofor (2009, ed.) *Who is an African? identity, citizenship and the making of the Africa-nation*. Adonis & Abbey Publishers.

Adler, Nils and Alsaafin, Linah (2023 July 30). Russia-Ukraine war updates: Drone attacks on Moscow and Crimea 'thwarted', *Aljazeera*. https://www.aljazeera.com/news/live blog/2023/7/30/russia-ukraine-war-live-drone-attack-on-moscow-thwarted-one-injured.

Africa News (2022, August 24). South Africa: Trade unions protest rising cost of living, record-high fuel prices. https://www.africanews.com/2022/08/24/south-africa-trade-unions-protest-rising-cost-of-living-record-high-fuel-prices//

Allimadi, Milton (2021). *Manufacturing hate: How Africa was demonized in western media*. Kendall Hunt Publishing Company.

Aris, Ben (2023, August 2). Niger coup threatens Nigeria-Morocco 30bcm gas pipeline project. BneIntellinews, https://www.intellinews.com/niger-coup-threatens-nigeria-morocco-30bcm-gas-pipeline-project-286426/

Arise News (2024, November 16). Zelensky: Ukraine war will end 'sooner' under Trump presidency. https://www.arise.tv/zelensky-ukraine-war-will-end-sooner-under-trump-presidency/

Arise News (2023, July 28). Putin promises free Russian grain shipments to 6 African countries.https://www.arise.tv/puti n-promises-free-russian-grain-shipments-to-6-african-countries/

Armstrong, Mark (2023, June 26). Russian FM Sergei Lavrov says Wagner mercenaries will continue to operate in Africa', *Euro News*. https://www.euronews.com/2023/06/26/russian-fm-sergei-lavrov-says-wagner-mercenaries-will-continue-to-operate-in-africa

Asadu, Chinedu (2024, January 24). Blinken pitches the US as an alternative to Russia's Wagner in Africa's troubled Sahel. *AP*. https://apnews.com/article/africa-sahel-blinken-wagner-coups-nigeria 8e14621ee695dda7097f89783a3c42a2

Barigazzi, Jacopo (2024, November 16). Positively surprised by call with Trump, Germany's Scholz says. Politico. https://www.politico.eu/article/positively-surprised-call-donald-trump-germany-olaf-scholz-vladimir-putin-nato-ukraine-war/

Bartlett, Kate. (2023, February 21). What joint drills with South African, Russian Navies mean for China. *Voice of America.* https://www.voanews.com/a/what-joint-drills-with-south-african-russian-navies-mean-for-china-/6972341.html

Bertrand, Natasha (2016, January 11). Putin: The deterioration of Russia's relationship with the West is the result of many 'mistakes'', *Yahoo Finance* https://finance.yahoo.com/news/putin-deterioration-russias-relationship-west-034104754.html?guce_referrer=aHR0cHM6Ly93d3cuZ29vZ2xlLmNvbS8&guce_referrer_sig=AQAAAFsKQ8F4XhDPjGDhUdp0YQ7g6M1MZuvZpTG8iJJek5cJkeCFpSXwIRPc1SPwUq9KHjKTtCD_nhyNyCANVis6CsrwsgLUfiRRFx9SdTSTH_bYl33Bdu2KBlGz-S3u-qDrvwXYkyJyQNbfqjkGWVz4caD9frSMf7tkCvA_01sfEHZk

Blenkinsop, Philip (2022, March 2). EU bars 7 Russian banks from SWIFT, but spares those in energy. *Reuters.* https://www.reuters.com/business/finance/eu-excludes-seven-russian-banks-swift-official-journal-2022-03-02/

Borger, Julian (2018, December 13). US unveils new Africa policy to counter 'predatory' Russia and China. *The Guardian* (UK). https://www.theguardian.com/us-news/2018/dec/13/us-john-bolton-africa-policy-russia-china

Brennan, David (2024, November 11). Russia prepares counteroffensive with 50,000 troops, potentially including North Koreans, sources say. ABC News. https://abcnews.go.com/International/russia-prepares-counteroffensive-50000-troops-potentially-including-north/story?id=115724508

Brunnstrom, David and Hunnicutt, Trevor (2023, September 19). Biden says U.S. forces would defend Taiwan in the event of a Chinese invasion. *Reuters* https://www.reuters.com/world/biden-says-us-forces-would-defend-taiwan-event-chinese-invasion-2022-09-18/#:~:text=WASHINGTON%2C%20Sept%2018%20(Reuters),those%20seeking%20an%20independent%20Taiwan.

Business & Human Rights Resource Centre. (2019, February11). Russia is increasing its influence in Africa through strategic investment in energy and minerals says analyst. https://www.business-humanrights.org/en/latest-news/russia-is-increasing-its-influence-in-africa-through-strategic-investment-in-energy-and-minerals-says-analyst/

Caprile, Anna and Pichon, Eric (2024, February,). Russia in Africa: An atlas (briefing). *European Parliament.* https://www.europarl.europa.eu/RegData/etudes/BRIE/2024/757654/EPRS_BRI(2024)757654_EN.pdf

Channels TV (2024, May 15). Nigeria's inflation rate soars to 33.69% in April 2024', https://www.channelstv.com/2024/05/15/breaking-nigerias-inflation-rate-soars-to-33-69-in-april 2024/#:~:text=Nigeria's%20inflation%20rate%20rose%20to,inflation%20rate%20which%20was%2033.20%25.

Chinweizu (1975). *The West and the rest of us: White predators, black slavers and the African elite.* Random House.

Chopra, Naimat (2023, May 5). Fuel, food, and fertilizer: the interwoven impacts of the Russia-Ukraine war. *Kleinman Centre for Energy Policy.* https://kleinmanenergy.upenn.edu/news-insights/fuel-food-and-fertilizer-the-interwoven-impacts-of-the-russia-ukraine-war/

Defence Web (2019, October 24,). Nigeria confirms order for a dozen Mi 35 helicopters from Russia. https://www.defenceweb.co.za/aerospace/aerospace-aerospace/niger-orders-a-dozen-mi-35-helicopters-from-russia/

Denise M Bostdorf (2008). *Proclaiming the Truman Doctrine: the Cold War call to arms.* Texas A&M University Press.

Douet, Marion (2023, March 28). Russia overtakes China as leading arms seller in sub-Saharan Africa', *Le Monde.* https://www.lemonde.fr/en/le-monde-africa/article/2023/03/28/russia-overtakes-china-as-

leading-arms-seller-in-sub-saharanafrica
_6021018_124.html#:~:text=Out%20with%20China
%2C%20back%20in,21%25%20over%20the%20previous
%20period.

Dorn, Sara (2024, September 24). Trump trashes Zelensky as 'greatest salesman on earth' as he visits U.S. Forbes. https://www.forbes.com/sites/saradorn/2024/09/24/tru mp-trashes-zelensky-as-greatest-salesman-on-earth-as-he-visits-us/

Duggal, Hanna (2023, July 17). As Russia exits grain deal, which countries will be affected? *Aljazeera.* https://www.aljazeera.com/news/2023/7/17/as-russia-exits-grain-deal-which-countries-will-be-affected#:~:text=The%20UN%20says%20the%20deal,UN %20calls%20high%2Dincome%20countries

ECA (2022, April 6). Afreximbank launches 4 billion US dollar Ukraine crisis adjustment Trade Financing Programme for Africa (UKAFPA)' https://www.uneca.org/stories/afrexi mbank-launches-4-billion-us-dollar-ukraine-crisis-adjustment-trade-financing-programme

Egypt Today (2024, January 28). Egypt, Russia trade exchange increases by 14% during 2023. https://www.egypttoday.com/Article/3/130006/Egypt-Russia-trade-exchange-increases-by-14-during-2023

Embassy of Nigeria in the Russian Federation, (n.d.). Bilateral relations'. https://nigerianembassy.ru/political-relation-2/political-relation-2/

Euronews (2024, September 8). US informs allies Iran transferred ballistic missiles to Russia to use in Ukraine war. https://www.euronews.com/2024/09/08/us-informs-allies-iran-transferred-ballistic-missiles-to-russia-to-use-in-ukraine-war

Fana BC (2023, December 20). Russian companies desirous to invest in Ethiopia. https://www.fanabc.com/english/russi an-companies-desirous-to-invest-in-ethiopia/

Fasanotti, Federica Saini (2022, February 8). Russia's Wagner Group in Africa: Influence, commercial concessions, rights violations, and counterinsurgency failure. *Brookings.* https://www.brookings.edu/articles/russias-wagner-group-in-africa-influence-commercial-concessions-rights-violations-and-counterinsurgency-failure/

Faulkner, Christopher (2022, June). Undermining democracy and exploiting clients: The Wagner Group's nefarious activities in Africa. *CTC Sentinel.* Volume 15, issue 6. CTC-SENTINEL-062022.pdf (westpoint.edu)

Felbab-Brown, Vanda (2023). What's ahead for the Wagner Group in Africa and the Middle East? *Brookings.* https://www.brookings.edu/articles/whats-ahead-for-the-wagner-group-in-africa-and-the-middle-east/

Forum Friends of the African Continental Free Trade Area (2022). Accelerating the implementation of the African Continental Free Trade Area agreement through public-private collaboration. *World Economic Forum.* .https://initiatives.weforum.org/forum-friends-of-the-african-continental-free-trade-area/home

France 24 (2023, July 28). Russia and Africa agree to promote 'multipolar world order', says Putin.https://www.france24.com/en/europe/20230728-russia-and-africa-agree-to-promote-multipolar-world-order-says-putin

Garamone, Jim (2023, February 4). F-22 safely shoots down Chinese spy balloon off South Carolina coast. *US Department of Defence.* https://www.defense.gov/News/News-Stories/Article/Article/3288543/f-22-safely-shoots-down-chinese-spy-balloon-off-south-carolina-coast/

Gibson, Joseph R. (2021). *How Europe and America are still underdeveloping Africa: Neocolonialism and the scramble for strategic resources in 21st century Africa* (independently published)

Gu, Xuewu (2022). China's engagement in Africa: Activities, effects and trends. Centre for Global Studies. https://www.cgs-bonn.de/cms/wp-content/uploads/2022/07/CGS-China_Africa_Study-2022.pdf

Gupte, Eklavya Griffin, Rosemary & Bowles, Alisdair (2019). Nigeria and Russia to 'widen and deepen' energy cooperation: Novak. S & P Global. https://www.spglobal.com/commodityinsights/en/market -insights/latest-news/natural-gas/102419-nigeria-and-russia-to-widen-and-deepen-energy-cooperation-novak

Hammer, Joshua (20024, May 3). What is Wagner doing in Africa? *The Atlantic* https://www.theatlantic.com/internati onal/archive/2024/05/wagner-africa-russia-mercenary/678258/

Hashash, Sara (2024, March 13). Egypt: Halt crackdown on people voicing concerns over economic crisis. *Amnesty International.*https://www.amnesty.org/en/latest/news/202 4/ 05/egypt-halt-crackdown-on-people-voicing-concerns-over-economic-crisis/

Hedenskog, Jakob (2018, December). Russia is stepping up its military cooperation in Africa. FOI, https://www.foi.se/rest- api/report/FOI %20MEMO%206604

History.Com (2024, May 16). Vietnam war. https:// www.history.com/topics/vietnam-war/vietnam-war-history

Horti, Samuel (2023, February 20). Ukraine war: Blinken says China might give weapons to Russia. *BBC.* https://www.bbc.com/news/world-us-canada-64695042

Husaini, Sa'eed (2024, July). We are producing, they are eating. *Africa is a Country.* https://africasacountry.com/2024/07/w e-are-producing-they-are-eating

IMF (2022, April). A new shock and little room to manoeuvre. https://www.imf.org/en/Publications/REO/SSA/Issues/ 2022/04/28/regional-economic-outlook-for-sub-saharan-africa-april-2022

ISPI (2023, July 13). Russia and China working "modus vivendi" in Africa. https://www.ispionline.it/en/publicatio

n/russia-and-china-working-modus-vivendi-in-africa 135837

Izuaka, Mary (2022, September 4). Nigeria to pay $496 million to settle Indian firm's claim over Ajaokuta steel. *Premium Times.* https://www.premiumtimesng.com/business/busin ess-news/552308-nigeria-to-pay-496-million-to-settle-indian-firms-claim-over-ajaokuta-steel.html?tztc=1

Jamasmie, Cecilia (2018, January 12). Alrosa buys stake in Angola's largest diamond deposit for $70 million. *Mining.com.* https://www.mining.com/alrosa-buys-stake-angolas-largest-diamond-deposit-70-million/#:~:text=Once%20finalized%2C%20Catoca%20w ill%20be,in%20Angola's%20Lunda%20Sul%20province.

Jones, Tom (2022, April 8). Nigeria abstains to vote in Russia's suspension from UN Human Rights Council. *Channels.* https://www.channelstv.com/2022/04/08/nigeria-abstains-to-vote-in-russias-suspension-from-un-human-rights-council/

Kaine, Tim (2017, July 28). A 21st century Truman Doctrine. *Brookings.* https://www.brookings.edu/articles/a-21st-century-truman-doctrine/

Keohane, Robert and Nye, Joseph (1977). Power and interdependence: World politics in transition. Little, Brown and Company.

Lüthi, Lorenz M. *(2008), The Sino-Soviet Split: Cold war in the Communist World.* Princeton University Press.

Meduza (2021, June 29). Prigozhin's criminal past, straight from the source: A complete translation of one of the court documents from the case that sent 'Putin's chef' to prison, four decades ago, *Meduza.* https://meduza.io/en/feature/2021/06/29/prigozhin-s-criminal-past-straight-from-the-source

Military Africa (2023, March 20), Despite war, Russia overtakes China as major arms supplier to Sub-Saharan Africa. https://www.military.africa/2023/03/despite-war-russia-overtakes-china-as-major-arms-supplier-to-sub-saharam-africa/

Mining Magazine (2022, March 21). GDI invests in Darwendale. https://www.miningmagazine.com/managem ent/news/1336668/gdi-invests-darwendale

Mlilo, Ndumiso (2022, August 11), Africans see through US ploy in Pelosi visit, *China Daily*. http://epaper.chinadaily.com.cn/a/202208/11/WS62f431 bca3109375516ee559.html

Mirovalev, Mansur (2024, November 15). Russia, Ukraine and the Koreas: Could Trump rock emerging wartime deals? AlJazeera, https://www.aljazeera.com/news/2024/11/15/rus sia-ukraine-and-the-koreas-could-trump-rock-emerging-wartime-deals

Mureithi, Carlos (2022, March 7), How African countries voted on Russia's invasion of Ukraine. *Quartz*. https://qz.com/africa/2138584/how-african-countries-voted-on-russias-invasion-of-ukraine

Murphy, Matt (2024, June 23). A year after mutiny, Kremlin controls Wagner remnants. https://www.bbc.com /news/articles/c4nn1p81q59o

Nanu, Maighna (2023, August 23), Russia paid $1 billion to Wagner group in one year, says Putin. *The Telegraph*. https://www.telegraph.co.uk/world-news/2023/06/27/russia-ukraine-war-latest-rivnopil-prigozhin-putin/

Natsa, Ruth Tene (2024, August 19). Russian engineers begin extensive assessment of Ajaokuta Steel Plant. *Business Day*. https://businessday.ng/news/article/russian-engineers-begin-extensive-assessment-of-ajaokuta-steel-plant/

NBC News (2005, April 25). Putin: Soviet collapse a 'genuine tragedy'. https://www.nbcnews.com/id/wbna7632057

Nova News (2023, December 2). Russia-Algeria agreement to produce one million tons of "green aluminium", https://www.agenzianova.com/en/news/accordo-russia-algeria-per-produrre-un-milione-di-tonnellate-di-alluminio-verde/

Oberdorfer, Dob (1978, March 4). The Superpowers and the Ogaden war. *Washington Post.* https://www.washingtonpost. com/archive/politics/1978/03/05/the-superpowers-and-the-ogaden-war/00f60ef2-01b4-4cd3-8c5f-e545df388def/

Okafor, Chiamaka (2023, July 23). European Union seeks more gas imports from Nigeria. *Premium Times,* https://www.premiumtimesng.com/business/business-news/544394-european-union-seeks-more-gas-imports-from-nigeria.html?tztc=1

Okafor, Chiamaka (2022, September 11), Russia-Ukraine War: Nigerian students lament plights seven months into conflict. *Premium Times.* https://www.premiumtimesng.com /news/headlines/553343-russia-ukraine-war-nigerian-students-lament-plights-seven-months-into-conflict.html?tztc=1

Oluyole, Francisca (2017, December 26). How Nigeria's largest industrial project failed. *Premium Times,* https://allafrica.com/stories/201712270020.html

Paraskova, Tsvetana (2018, May 24). Nigerian firm to partner with Rosneft to develop 21 African oil assets. *Oil Price.* https://oilprice.com/Latest-Energy-News/World-News/Nigerian-Firm-To-Partner-With-Rosneft-To-Develop-21-African-Oil-Assets.html

Patel, Vedant (2022, November 4). Yevgeniy Prigozhin's Africa-wide disinformation campaign. *US Department of State,* https://www.state.gov/disarming-disinformation/yevgeniy-prigozhins-africa-wide-disinformation-campaign/

Patta, Debora (2023, July 28,). Russia-Africa summit hosted by Putin draws small crowd, reflecting Africa's changing mood on Moscow, *CBS News.* https://www.cbsnews.com/news/russia-africa-summit-vladimir-putin-ukraine-war-wagner-group/

Paquette, Danielle (2019, October 25), As the U.S. looks elsewhere, Russia seeks a closer relationship with Africa. *Washington Post.* https://www.washingtonpost.com/world/africa/as-the-us-looks-elsewhere-russia-seeks-a-closer-relationship-with-africa/2019/10/25/7e329124-f69e-11e9-b2d2-1f37c9d82dbb_story.html

Pham, J. Peter (2014, March 14), Russia's return to Africa', *Atlantic Council,* https://www.atlanticcouncil.org/comment ary/article/russia-s-return-to-africa/

Plaut, Martin (2018, November 3), The Chinese and Soviets had a bigger role in supporting apartheid than we previously knew', *Quartz.* https://qz.com/africa/1449906/china-soviets-backed-both-south-africa-apartheid-and-liberation

Pottinger, Brian (2022, November 11), Why South Africa is siding with Russia: The ANC can't afford to be virtuous. *Unherd,* https://unherd.com/2022/11/why-south-africa-is-siding-with-russia/

Rampe, William (2023, May 23). What Is Russia's Wagner Group doing in Africa? *Council on Foreign Relations.* https://www.cfr.org/in-brief/what-russias-wagner-group-doing-africa

Ray, Charles (2023, April 13), South Africa's Naval Exercises with China and Russia: Causes for concern? *Foreign Policy Research Institute.* https://www.fpri.org/article/2023/04/so uth-africas-naval-exercises-with-china-and-russia-cause-for-concern/

Resnick, Danielle (2022, February 25). What does the war in Ukraine mean for Africa? *Brookings Institution.* https://www.brookings.edu/articles/what-does-the-war-in-ukraine-mean-for-africa/

Roelf, Wendell (2023, December 11), South Africa picks Russia's Gazprombank as PetroSA refinery partner. *Reuters.* https://www.reuters.com/business/energy/south-africa-selects-russias-gazprombank-partner-petrosa-refinery-2023-12-11/

Rubinstein, Alvin Z (1971). Lumumba University assessment. Problems of Communism cited in *Wikipedia.* Africa-Soviet

Union Relations. https://en.wikipedia.org/wiki/Africa%E2%80%93Soviet_Union_relations

Ruedy, John (1992). *Modern Algeria: the origins and development of a nation.* Indiana University Press.

Reuters (2024, October 30). Europe will pay a 'big price,' Trump warns on tariffs. https://www.reuters.com/world/europe-will-pay-big-price-trump-warns-tariffs-2024-10-30/

Reuters, (2023, June 18), Putin rebuts key elements of African peace plan for Ukraine. https://www.reuters.com /world/europe/african-leaders-arrive-ukraine-talks-with-russias-putin-2023-06-17/

Reuters (2022, June 9). Afromet exits Zimbabwe platinum mine project. Mining.com. https://www.mining.com/web/afromet-exits-zimbabwe-platinum-mine-project/

Reuters, (2021, April 5). Putin signs law that could keep him in Kremlin until 2036. https://www.reuters.com /article/idUSKBN2BS18V/

Reuters (2019, October 25). Russia signs deal to supply Nigeria with 12 attack helicopters: RIA. *Reuters.* https://www.reuters.com/article/instant-article/idUKL5N278554/

SAIPEC (2022, 16 September). Sub-Saharan Africa to drive Africa's oil and gas project opportunities, investments. https://saipec-event.com/saipec-news/sub-saharan-africa-drive-africas-oil-gas-project-opportunities-investments#:~:text=Senegal%20has%20oil%20and%20gas,were%20discovered%20in%20the%20area

Sauer, Pjotr (2023, June 23). Wagner chief accuses Moscow of lying to public about Ukraine. *The Guardian.* https://www.theguardian.com/world/2023/jun/23/wagner-chief-accuses-moscow-of-lying-to-public-about-ukraine-yevgeny-prigozhin

Saunders, Michael (2023, September1), Russia drives Switzerland closer to NATO. *IISS.*

https://www.iiss.org/en/online-analysis/military-balance/2023/09/russia-drives-switzerland-closer-to-nato/

Shehu, Garba (2019, October 26), The takeaways from Buhari's visit to Russia. *The Cable*. https://www.thecable.ng/the-takeaways-from-buharis-visit-to-russia/

Siegle, Joseph (2023, September 6). Inflection point for Africa–Russia Relations after Prigozhin's Death. *Africa Centre for Strategic Studies*, https://africacenter.org/spotlight/inflection-point-for-africa-russia-relations-after-prigozhins-death/

Singh, Tanupriya (2023, September 26), Ghana witnesses fresh protests against rising cost of living. *Peoples Dispatch*, https://peoplesdispatch.org/2023/09/26/ghana-witnesses-fresh-protests-against-rising-cost-of-living/

Smith, Elliot (2023, July 17). Wagner's failed rebellion could hit the Kremlin's ambitions for a 'pro-Russian state' in Africa. *CNBC*. https://www.cnbc.com/2023/07/17/wagners-rebellion-could-hit-kremlins-pro-russian-state-in-africa.html

Stark, Vicky, (2022, May 10). South Africa poised to exploit growing demand for platinum group metals. *VOA News*. https://www.voanews.com/a/south-africa-poised-to-exploit-growing-demand-for-platinum-group-metals-/6565894.html

Stone, Mike and Pamuk, Humeyra (2024, November 18). Biden allows Ukraine to use US arms to strike inside Russia. Reuters. https://www.reuters.com/world/biden-lifts-ban-ukraine-using-us-arms-strike-inside-russia-2024-11-17/

Tan, Yvette & Molloy, David (2022, August 3). Taiwan: Nancy Pelosi meets president Tsai to Beijing's fury', *BBC*. https://www.bbc.com/news/world-asia-62398029

Tass (2023, July26), History of relations of Soviet Union, Russia with African countries. *Tass*. https://tass.com/politics/1652463

The Conversation (2022, April 13). Russia-Ukraine crisis highlights Africa's need to diversify its wheat sources.

https://theconversation.com/russia-ukraine-crisis-highlights-africas-need-to-diversify-its-wheat-sources-181173#:~:text=Between%202018%20and%202020%2C%20Africa,sources%20for%20two%20key%20reasons

The New York Times (1964, May 17). De Beers ends pact to sell Soviet gems. https://www.nytimes.com/1964/05/17/archives/de-beers-ends-pact-to-sell-soviet-gems.html

TRT Afrika (2023, June 30), Russia to support Africa's inclusion in UN Security Council. https://www.trtafrika.com/world/russia-to-support-africas-inclusion-in-un-security-council-13844344

Ulimwengu, John (2023, May 31). The impact of Russia-Ukraine conflict on food and nutrition security in Africa: A call for a more resilient African food system. *Food Security Portal.* (Facilitated by IFPRI), https://ssa.foodsecurityportal.org/node/2431

Vernou, Axel de (2023, April 27). Africa is Russia's new resource outlet. *The National Interest.* https://nationalinterest.org/feature/africa-russia%E2%80%99s-new-resource-outlet-206432

VOA News (2023, March 19), Gunmen kill 9 Chinese at mine in Central African Republic. https://www.voanews.com/a/gunmen-kill-9-chinese-at-mine-in-central-african-republic-/7012194.html

Volpi, Cristiano (2024, April 3). Russia Strengthens ties with Ethiopia through healthcare and education Initiatives' *Africa24.IT/En.* https://africa24.it/en/2024/04/03/russia-expands-influence-in-ethiopia-with-health-and-education-initiatives/

Vurren, Van Hennie (2018), Apartheid Guns and Money: A Tale of Profit. C Hurst & Co.

Wheeler, Tom (2009, July 8). Russian president Medvedev's visit to Africa, June 2009. *SAIIA@90 Years,* https://saiia.org.za/research/russian-president-medvedevs-visit-to-africa-june-2009/

Willers, David (2023, June 30), South Africa, Russia and ten days that shook the world: Pretoria's love affair with

Moscow. *Litnet*. https://www.litnet.co.za/south-africa-russia-and-ten-days-that-shook-the-world-pretorias-love-affair-with-moscow/

Wintour, Patrick (2023, July 20). What was the Black Sea grain deal and why did it collapse? *The Guardian*. https://www.theguardian.com/world/2023/jul/20/what-was-the-black-sea-grain-deal-and-why-did-it-collapse

Wiseman, Paul (2024, September 27). Trump favours huge new tariffs. How do they work?, PBS News, https://www.pbs.org/newshour/economy/trump-favors-huge-new-tariffs-how-do-they-work

Wyatt, Caroline (2001, June 16). Bush and Putin: Best of friends. *BBC News*, http://news.bbc.co.uk/2/hi/1392791.stm

Xinhua (2022, February 2). Russia to invest 1.2 bln USD to build fertilizer factory in Angola. https://english.news.cn/europe/20220202/a5549bb3996948bca8245514aa4332ef/c.html

Index

A

Abia State, 11
Adibe, Jideofor Patrick C, 37, 72, 79, 94, 99
Adonis & Abbey Publishers, 17, 18, 19, 21, 27, 99
Africa Centre for Strategic Studies, Washington, 63
Africa Corps, 86
African Continental Free Trade Area, 68, 92, 104
African Export-Import Bank, 41
African Import-Export Bank, 68, 92
African Union Commission, 41
African Writers' Series, 18
Ajaokuta Steel Company, 33, 35
Algerian War of Independence, 29
Aliegba, Eugene, 7
Alroser, 51
Amali, Shamsudeen, 9
Ankomah, Baffour, 18
Anowai, Dennis, 9
Apartheid, 32, 113
Azi, Ufaruna Sarah, 9

B

Babatope, Ebenezer, 12

Balewa, Tafawa, 32
Biafran Army, 11
Biden, Joe, 75, 79, 94, 102, 112
Blinken, Anthony, 49, 64, 100, 106
Boer War, 31
Boko Haram, 39, 54
Bolton, John, 49
BRIC, 17
Brookings Institution, 22, 23, 76, 77, 99, 110

C

Camp David Accords, 31
Centre for Development Research, Copenhagen, 15
Chase, James Hadley, 13, 14
Chatham House, 23, 74, 76, 77, 78
City University, London, 17
Cold War, 23, 38, 57, 59, 74, 75, 76, 78, 79, 87, 96, 99, 103
Congolese National Movement, 30
Cross-conditionalities, 15

D

Dandago, Kabiru Isa, 9
De Beers, 32, 112
Derg, 31
Durrants, 18

E

Economic Community of Central African States, 41
E-International Relations, 23, 99
Ekwusigo Local Government Area of Anambra, 11, 12
Elaigwu, J Isawa, 9, 19, 21
Ethiopia-Russia Business Forum, 52
Ethio-Somali War, 31
European Union, 65, 74, 93, 108

F

Fourth Dimension Publishers, 15

G

Gazprom, 40, 50, 52, 55
Global Civilisation Initiative, 61
Global Development Initiative, 61
Global Security Initiative, 61
Global Steel Holdings Limited, 35
Goldman Sachs, 17
Great Dykes Investment, 50
Gumede, William, 43

H

Hashimu, Hashimu Shuaibu, 9
Hassan Liman, Sa'adatu, 7
Hassan, Samia Suluhu, 65

H

Heinemann, 18
Horn of Africa, 31
Human Development Index, 68

I

Intergovernmental Authority on Development, 41

J

Jacko, David Sunday, 8
Jirgi, Abigail, 22
Jonathan, Goodluck, 22

K

Keohane, Robert, 24, 106
Khrushchev, Nikita, 37, 59, 60, 89
Kitissou, Marcel, 19

L

Lagi, Theo, 7
Lenin, Vladimir, 30, 88
Lukoil, 39, 50, 52, 55

M

Maghreb, 41, 54
Make America Great Again, 93
Makele, Mamman Ali, 12
Mariam, Mengistu Haile, 31
Marxist-Leninist ideology, 59
Mastercard, 67, 92
Mazrui Ali, 19, 21, 99
Mbadiwe, K.O., 12

www.ingramcontent.com/pod-product-compliance
Lightning Source LLC
Chambersburg PA
CBHW050843270326
41930CB00019B/3445